UNLEASHING AMERICA'S POTENTIAL

A PRO-GROWTH, PRO-FAMILY TAX SYSTEM FOR THE TWENTY-FIRST CENTURY

The National Commission on
Economic Growth and Tax Reform

ST. MARTIN'S GRIFFIN 🦁 NEW YORK

UNLEASHING AMERICA'S POTENTIAL
Copyright © 1996 by the Fund for the Study of Economic Growth and Tax
Reform. All rights reserved. Printed in the United States of America. No part of
this book may be used or reproduced in any manner whatsoever without written
permission except in the case of brief quotations embodied in critical articles or
reviews. For information, address St. Martin's Press, 175 Fifth Avenue,
New York, N.Y. 10010.

Book design by Gretchen Achilles

ISBN 0-312-14618-3

First St. Martin's Griffin Edition
10 9 8 7 6 5 4 3 2 1

CONTENTS

FOREWORD

LETTER TO THE AMERICAN PEOPLE

BY BOB DOLE AND NEWT GINGRICH

"Taxation without representation is tyranny." Those are the words that helped to ignite the American Revolution over two centuries ago.

As we approach the twenty-first century, the crescendo for tax reform continues to build, year after year, election after election. Americans have looked at a tax system constantly increasing in both rates and complexity, and concluded that taxation with representation wasn't so good either.

The current tax system is indefensible. It is overly complex, burdensome, and severely limits economic opportunity for all Americans.

We made clear on the very first day of the 104th Congress that our top priority would be to change the status quo and to bring fundamental change to America. And we agreed that there is no status quo that needs more fundamental change than our tax system.

We envision:

- A tax system that is fairer, flatter, and simpler.

- A tax system that promotes, rather than punishes, job creation.

- A tax system that eliminates unnecessary paperwork burdens on America's businesses.

- A tax system that recognizes the fact that our families are performing the most important work of our society.

- A tax system that provides incentives for Americans who save for the future in order to build a better life for themselves and their families

- A tax system that allows Americans, especially the middle-class, to keep more of what they earn, but that raises enough money to fund a leaner, more efficient federal government.

- A tax system that allows Americans to compute their taxes easily, without the need for a lawyer, an accountant—or both.

To help make this vision a reality, we named Jack Kemp, one of America's most innovative thinkers on economic policy, to head the National Commission on Economic Growth and Tax Reform—a commission that included thirteen other outstanding Americans.

The entire commission worked diligently for the past several months, holding twelve public hearings in eight cities, while constantly thinking about how to create a better tax system.

Their final report is guaranteed to stimulate this important national dialogue. It will surely serve as a catalyst for congressional hearings and debate. We hope that it will also trigger conversations around kitchen tables, water coolers, and in town hall meetings across the country.

We invite all of you who read this report to write to us with your thoughts on its recommendations and conclusions, and to share with us other suggestions on how we can create a tax system that promotes economic growth and opportunity for all Americans.

Senate Majority Leader
Bob Dole

House Speaker
Newt Gingrich

PREFACE

A NEW LEVEL OF THINKING

BY EDWIN J. FEULNER

"They act like all that money is *born* in Washington, D.C." Perhaps no comment has better summarized the problem with our nation's capital than this observation by Ed Zorinsky, the late Democratic Senator from Nebraska. And nowhere is this governmental conceit expressed more destructively than in the workings and effects of our Internal Revenue Code.

Many previous attempts at tax reform have been marred by the inside-the-beltway assumption that the wealth of the nation belongs to its government. This has perpetuated the "tin-cup syndrome"—an environment in which the political competition over scarce resources replaces the economic competition that generates growth, creates jobs, and spurs innovation and productivity. As a consequence, the tax code has become increasingly politicized over the years, and is seen less as a simple tool for raising revenue than as an instrument for social and economic engineering. In turn, this has spawned a virtual industry of tax specialists and special interest lobbyists, while exponentially increasing the complexity of the code.

The National Commission on Economic Growth and Tax Reform set out with a different set of assumptions. We began with the belief that the purpose of the tax code is to raise money while leaving citizens as free as possible to pursue the American dream. Our charge from Senate Leader Dole and Speaker Gingrich was clear: Listen first and learn from the American people. We listened to ordinary taxpayers in hearings around the country. What we heard was a great deal of frustration, concern, and, yes, anger with the current system. Our hope has been to channel those frustrations into a set of concrete principles and recommendations that any new tax reform legislation must follow if it is to meet the needs and expectations of the American people.

From June until September 1995, we heard from a cross-section of American taxpayers in Boston, Omaha, Charlotte, Palo Alto, south-central Los Angeles, Harlem, Cleveland, and Washington, D.C. We listened to and learned from family farmers and high-tech entrepreneurs, small businessmen and women, medium-sized and large manufacturers, governors and mayors, congressmen and senators, leading economists and local activists.

Unlike previous "reform" commissions, our activities were financed without a dime from the American taxpayer. Expenses were met through private contributions from more than 1,500 donors. The fourteen commissioners received no compensation for the long hours and hard work, save the tremendous reward of knowing their sacrifices would help shape American history. This is an extraordinary group of American citizens who have demonstrated through untold hours of hearings, deliberations, and study their dedication to chart a course to a freer, more prosperous America. We believe we have set that course.

In 1941, in a famous essay for *Life* magazine, Henry Luce anticipated that the twentieth century would be remembered as the American Century. The decades and events that followed—the defeat of Nazi Germany, the collapse of communism, the expansion of American influence abroad—bore this prediction out. Today, many citizens fear they see that era of American preeminence slipping away. The optimism and boundlessness that have always defined America are seen by some as fond but faded relics to be quietly folded away.

This report reflects the firm conviction that America can do better. None of the members of this commission would have accepted this challenge if they did not believe in the possibility of real progress and real reform.

Albert Einstein observed that "The problems of today cannot be solved at the same level of thinking on which they were created." We have concluded that the complex tax code of the twentieth century is poorly suited for dealing with the complex world of the twenty-first. The vision outlined in the following pages cannot be realized by simply rearranging the deck chairs on the *Titanic* we call our current tax code. A brand-new tax code, modeled on the principles and recommendations proposed in this report, can chart the economic waters ahead and launch our country on its voyage toward the next American century.

Vice Chairman
National Commission on Economic Growth and Tax Reform
Edwin J. Feulner

INTRODUCTION

SETTING THE EAGLE FREE

BY JACK KEMP

"In short, it is a paradoxical truth that tax rates are too high today and tax revenues are too low, and the soundest way to raise the revenues in the long run is to cut the rates now....The purpose of cutting taxes now is not to incur a budget deficit, but to achieve the more prosperous, expanding economy which can bring a budget surplus."

JOHN F. KENNEDY
Economic Club of New York
December 14, 1962

These words of President Kennedy were a great inspiration to me as the tax reform movement was launched in the early 1980s with the Kemp/Roth tax cut. Kennedy's vision and courage can serve as examples for all Americans as we struggle to make this nation better for our children and grandchildren. His remarks at the Economic Club of New York ring as true today as they did in 1962.

At the first meeting of our commission back in June, I held up a blank sheet of paper and said, "This is what we start with." That was our charge: Senate Majority Leader Bob Dole and House Speaker Newt Gingrich appointed the National Commission on Economic Growth and Tax Reform to study the current tax code, listen to the suggestions and ideas of people from around the country, and submit to Congress our recommendations for comprehensive reform. A very diverse and dedicated group of fourteen people, with the help of an invaluable, overworked, and underpaid staff, set out to design an entirely new tax system for America's twenty-first century—one which would promise a booming economy, promote job creation, and ensure the greatest possible opportunity for all Americans to work, save, invest, and reach their potential. We operated under the premise that an economic growth rate of 2.5 percent is unacceptable to the American people.

This commission was empowered not merely to offer superficial reforms, to trim a rate here and close a loophole there, but to begin with a *tabula rasa* and map out a totally new tax structure for America's next century. We also wanted to help inform the whole world, particularly the emerging democracies, that the goal of tax policy is raising revenue, not redistribution of wealth.

Our nation has arrived at a unique moment in history. With the passing of the Cold War, we are standing at the edge of a new millennium with extraordinary possibilities. Our country is poised to help lead the world into a new era of economic growth fueled by an information-age technological revolution that can yield unparalleled expansion in jobs, productivity, innovation, and prosperity. We must embrace this opportunity and challenge. However, such an embrace will prove difficult, perhaps impossible, if we remain saddled with our current tax code. The current system is indefensible: It is riddled with special interest tax breaks, and it overtaxes both labor and capital. We must construct a tax system that reflects our highest values and unleashes our greatest potential.

The comments and concerns we heard from the American people over the last several months, coupled with a systematic review of the current tax code, helped us establish certain principles that guided us to our conclusions. Surely, a fair and simple tax code must generate sufficient revenue for the federal government to carry out its legitimate tasks. Second, it must not place a tax burden on those members of society least able to bear one. And, perhaps most important of all, it must not restrict the innovative and entrepreneurial capacities of Americans upon which rising living standards and our general prosperity so greatly depend. Our proposals are in keeping with these principles.

Wildly excessive and unjust taxes have locked away access to capital and credit necessary for low-income Americans to launch the next generation of entrepreneurship. Today, sadly, we see the American people's sense of dynamism and hope, their ability to strive and compete, diminished by a tax code which penalizes success, retards investment, and sends capital fleeing overseas. The commission is united in the belief that only a pro-growth tax code can restore America's confidence at home and her greatness abroad. We want a tax code and an overall economy that will liberate the American dream and remove the barriers to upward social and economic mobility. The American ethos of entrepreneurship and optimism made America great once before. We believe these proposals will bolster that ethos again and help restore integrity and honesty to our system.

The author John Gardner has observed that there are many contributing factors to the rise of civilization—accidents of resources, geography, and military power. But whatever other ingredients comprise the greatness of nations, he writes, "There occurs at breathtaking moments in history an exhilarating burst of energy and motivation, of hope and zest and imagination, and a severing of the bonds that normally hold in check the full release of human possibilities. A door is opened, and the caged eagle soars."

That eagle, the symbol of our nation, represents the creative spirit, talents, and aspirations of the American people. The charge of this commission and the intent of our recommendations is to open the door and help set that eagle in all of us free.

Chairman
National Commission on Economic Growth and Tax Reform
Jack Kemp

PART ONE
THE REPORT OF
THE COMMISSION

The National Commission on Economic Growth and Tax Reform recommends to the Congress and to the President of the United States that the current Internal Revenue Code be repealed in its entirety.

The present system is beyond repair—it is impossibly complex, outrageously expensive, overly intrusive, economically destructive, and manifestly unfair.

It is time to replace this failed system with a new simplified tax system for the twenty-first century: a single low rate, taxing income only once with a generous personal exemption and full deductibility of the payroll tax for America's working men and women.

This system will reduce the tax burden on middle-income people and will help remove the barriers that keep low-income Americans from reaching their fullest potential.

These changes, once in place, should be sealed with a guarantee of long-term stability, requiring a two-thirds vote of the U.S. Congress to raise the rate.

This new system is predicated on a commitment to expanding growth and opportunity. We believe the changes we propose will help to nearly double the rate of economic growth.

A stronger economy will create more jobs, raise family incomes, expand ownership and entrepreneurship, and ensure greater opportunity for our children and grandchildren. It will also produce additional revenues for balancing the budget and reducing the burden of national debt.

IMAGINE AN AMERICA...

WITH A PRO-GROWTH,

PRO-FAMILY TAX CODE

The principles and recommendations contained in this report comprise the "Tax Test"—the standard to which any new tax system must be held. We ask that Congress not pass and the President not sign any tax legislation that fails to pass this test. And we encourage the public to use the goals and guidelines we offer as a road map through the coming national debate on tax reform.

Our aim: to introduce a new system of taxation that brings out the best in the American character, that plays to our strengths and not our weaknesses, that speaks to our hopes and not our fears. Our recommendations are based on a vision of America that places the individual—not the government—at the center of society:

- We believe that government does not create opportunity; citizens do, if government will get out of their way.

- We believe that government is not the engine of economic growth; it is, more frequently, the monkey wrench in the machine.

- We believe that taxpayers' earnings and savings—their property—are not assets on loan from the government. The government is power on loan from the people.

One of the most serious shortcomings of previous attempts at tax reform has been the inability of average Americans to make their voices heard above the chorus of special interests. We have tried a radically different approach: Listening to the people first.

In his first debate with Stephen Douglas, Abraham Lincoln remarked that "with public sentiment, nothing can fail; without it nothing can succeed." We believe that any major legislative attempt to replace the current tax code will falter unless it is first preceded by a national debate on what the new system should look like.

Many previous attempts to reform public policy have failed to achieve their aims because they substituted closed meetings for democratic dialogue, focusing too much on expert analysis and too little on citizens' concerns. By including the public in the deliberations over tax reform, this commission seeks to build broad-based consensus behind a new tax system for America's next millennium.

It was with this spirit that the commission held cross-country public hearings—from the historic home of the Boston Tea Party to the heart of south-central L.A. At every hearing in every city, we asked people to tell us what they saw as the problems with the current system and the goals any reform plan should achieve.

- **In Omaha,** farmers pleaded for simpler filing and the freedom to pass family farms on to their children without fear of federal confiscation.

- **In the Silicon Valley**, high-tech entrepreneurs told of the countless ideas conceived but never born because of a scarcity of investment capital.

- **In south-central Los Angeles**, small business–owners voiced frustrations at not being able to expand or hire new workers because of a tax bite that eats away their profits.

- **And in Harlem,** inner-city entrepreneurs expressed both bitterness and bewilderment at a tax code which sucked revenues out of their neighborhoods while preventing investment from flowing in.

In our nation's capital, we heard from elected officials in both the House and the Senate who have for many years been leaders in tax reform. Because of their tireless public service, tax reform is a priority issue on the nation's agenda.

We also heard from many of the finest economists in the country who shared their knowledge and research with us at every hearing.

After our hearings, we held a series of working sessions to analyze what we had heard and to begin discussing our recommendations for change. During one of our working sessions, the commissioners put aside the charts and graphs for a moment, stepped back, and tried to imagine what kind of world they would like America's next generation to grow up in. We were asked to think about how replacing the tax code might help bring that world about:

- Imagine an America enjoying a decade of economic growth at nearly twice the present rate—creating jobs, expanding opportunities, and lifting living standards for all.

- Imagine an America in which more dreams born in basements and garages grow into multimillion-dollar businesses because abundant capital seeks out good ideas, and entrepreneurs and investors are confident that their risk-taking will be rewarded.

- Imagine an America where it is easier to get a job than to get on welfare, and where our inner cities share in America's growth and prosperity. Imagine these neighborhoods ringing out, not with sirens in the night, but with the sounds of new storefronts being opened and new businesses being built.

- Imagine an America where home ownership and higher education are within the reach of every American so that each citizen owns a stake in the system and shares a common interest and responsibility for its future.

- Imagine an America where young couples aren't asked to take a tax hit in order to exchange their marriage vows, and where young families can save for their future without being punished for their thrift.

- Imagine an America where Americans have enough to give, not just to and through their government, but to their churches, synagogues, their charities, and neighbors in need.

- Imagine an America where the I.R.S. becomes the "TPA"—a Taxpayer Protection Agency—to ensure that no one pays more than is owed. Imagine a customer-friendly approach to raising revenue, based on a belief in the basic honesty of the American people, and treats them with dignity and respect.

We believe that replacing our tax system with one that is simpler and fairer can help to make these American dreams come true.

America was not founded on envy or resentment. The American idea was never to keep everyone at the same mean level, but to give everyone the chance to rise as high as his or her effort, initiative, and God-given talent would allow. It was a promise of equal opportunity, not of end results: the confidence that whatever you aspired to become—be it artist, inventor, or entrepreneur—you could make it happen here.

A new tax system, as envisioned in the following pages of this report, can take a first step toward renewing that sense of hope and possibility by unleashing a cascade of benefits, beginning with greater economic growth, lower interest rates, and expanded job opportunities for working Americans.

Dramatic change never is easy, and complicated issues will arise in the transition that must be handled wisely and with care. We are confident that the Congress and the President will treat transition issues with due diligence and sensitivity.

We urge the Congress and the President to base any new legislation on the principles and recommendations submitted in this report. Furthermore, we urge the President to appoint a presidential task force or commission to bring the recommendations offered by this congressionally appointed commission to the next level of public debate.

AT THE BOILING POINT

"My grandmother used to tell me the folk tale of the frog," recounted Commissioner Herman Cain of his childhood in Atlanta, Georgia. "If you put a frog in a pot of hot water, he would jump right out. But if you put him in a pot of cool water and gradually turned up the heat, he wouldn't notice the rising temperature and would eventually boil to death."

The American taxpayer is in hot water. Escalating marginal tax rates, increasing complexity, and advancing intrusiveness have created a system that has reached the boiling point. Over the years, Americans have surrendered more and more of their freedom to higher taxes. The result has not been to enhance economic security or to close the gulf between rich and poor. Instead, it has led to fewer jobs, slow economic growth, diminished hope and opportunity, an erosion of trust and confidence in government, and an ebbing of the American spirit of enterprise. It is a history that echoes James Madison's warning that "There are more instances of the abridgment of the freedom of the people by gradual and silent encroachments...than by violent and sudden usurpation."

The time has passed for incremental reform. The problems with the current system have grown too deeply entrenched to be solved with quick fixes and cosmetic repairs.

We believe the current tax code cannot be revised, should not be reinvented, and must not be retained. Therefore, the commission is unanimous: It is time to throw out the seven-million-word mess of tax laws and regulations and begin anew.

Marc Negri of Santa Rosa, California, wrote to tell us that "The current system is so wrong and such a disincentive to the everyday worker that it cannot be saved." Lawrence Madsen of Mills, Wyoming, prepares peoples' taxes for a living, and yet wrote: "I am so disgusted with the [system] that I must urge you to completely abolish the Internal Revenue Code and start over." A retired couple from Astor, Florida, was even more blunt: "The current tax structure is way out of date with the real world, too complicated with too many loopholes. We say dump it!"

Americans' eagerness for real change reflects in part their frustration with a system that in the past forty years has seen thirty-one "significant" reforms and an astounding four hundred additional "revisions" through public laws. And yet the tax code is more complex, more costly, and more economically destructive than ever. This is the story of how we got here.

THE ROAD TO TAX OPPRESSION

The New York Times, in a 1909 editorial opposing the very first income tax, predicted: "When men get in the habit of helping themselves to the property of others, they cannot easily be cured of it." The history of our tax code, in economic terms, mirrors the course of most addictions: advancing dependence, diminished returns, and deteriorating health of the afflicted.

Supporters of the Sixteenth Amendment touted the income tax as the rich man's burden—forcing "the Carnegies, the Vanderbilts, the Morgans, and the Rockefellers" to pay while sparing the middle class from pain. Indeed, after the income tax was enacted in 1913, fewer than 2 percent of American families were required to file a tax return. Rates ranged from 1 to 7 percent—with the highest rate applying only to Americans who had the equivalent of $7.7 million in income in today's terms.

The rates did not stay that low for long. In 1916 the top rate doubled. A year later, on the eve of America's entry into World War I, it soared to 67 percent. With the Second World War, the rate was raised to 94 percent. In the 1950s the top rate remained at the sky-high level of more than 90 percent. President Kennedy initiated legislation that cut the top rate to 70 percent, but it was not until the Reagan growth years that the top rate was lowered dramatically to 28 percent. Under the current administration, the rate has resumed its ascent, with combined federal taxes pushing the top rate above 40 percent, including Medicare taxes and phase-outs.

With every attempt by politicians to "soak the rich," the water mark has risen on the middle class. Author Frank Chodorov has summed up the incremental march of encroaching taxation: "At first it was the incomes of corporations, then of rich citizens, then of well-provided widows and opulent workers, and finally the wealth of housemaids and the tips of waitresses." Congress expanded the income tax into the ranks of the middle class for the same reason Willie Sutton robbed banks: That's where the money is.

This shift was mainly achieved by gradually multiplying the number of taxpayers required to file income tax returns and by raising average tax rates on ordinary citizens. Until World War II, the average tax rate (that is, the total tax paid divided by income) on a family with a 1991 income of $50,000 never rose above 4 percent. Since World War II, it has never fallen below 14 percent.

Marginal rates on the middle class have risen even more dramatically. Marginal rates are the "tax bracket" rates that apply to any extra dollar of income—such as raises, overtime, bonuses, or a second family income. The marginal middle-class tax rate never rose above 8 percent prior to World War II. Since then, it has never fallen below 22 percent, rising as high as 33 percent during the high-inflation, bracket creep years of the 1970s.

Today, there are three principal defects of our income tax system that must be fixed immediately:

- **Economically Destructive:** Steeply graduated tax rates on both labor and capital destroy jobs, penalize saving and investment, and punish personal efforts to get ahead through hard work and education.

- **Impossibly Complex:** The mind-boggling complexity of the current tax code imposes an unacceptable burden on taxpayers and a huge cost on the economy.

- **Overly Intrusive:** The vast enforcement powers conferred on the I.R.S. are increasingly seen as infringements of privacy and personal freedom.

ECONOMICALLY DESTRUCTIVE

In the famous Supreme Court case, *McCulloch* v. *Maryland,* Chief Justice Marshall wrote: "The power to tax involves the power to destroy." Some of the ways in which the current tax code destroys our economic vitality include:

- High marginal tax rates that weaken the link between effort and reward, depress productivity, and kill jobs.

- Multiple layers of taxation on work, saving, and investment that dry up new capital for investment.

- Capital gains taxes that act as a barrier to capital formation—preventing the flow of investment to new enterprises and would-be entrepreneurs.

- An "alternative minimum tax" that imposes immense compliance costs on businesses, sapping resources that could otherwise be put to constructive use.

- Double taxation of corporate income that shrinks business investment and encourages companies to take on extra debt.

- Estate and gift taxes that force families to sell their businesses or family farms.

A fundamental principle of economics is that the more you tax something, the less you get of it. And if you tax success, you get less success. The current confiscatory system begs the questions: Why work harder if each extra dollar earns you less? Why save for tomorrow when spending today is cheaper? Why dream bigger, when little dreams are less expensive? The disillusioned answer of many Americans is simply: Why bother?

But the current system does not simply sap the initiative and aspirations of individual taxpayers, it undermines the economic strength of our nation as a whole. As President Kennedy once observed: "An economy hampered with high tax rates will never produce enough revenue to balance the budget, just as it will never produce enough output and enough jobs."

High marginal tax rates combined with multiple taxation of work, saving, and investment act as a "double-barreled shotgun aimed at the American economy," accountant Ted Krauss told the commission during a hearing in Washington. The price tag was estimated by Professor Dale Jorgenson of Harvard University, who told the commission that the income level in the United States could be 15 percent to 20 percent higher than today if these biases did not exist.

This translates to losses of as much as $4,000 to $6,000 per year for typical middle-income families. The tremendous economic drain caused by an antiwork, antisaving, and antigrowth tax system does not even take into account the enormous waste of resources—the time, money, and brainpower—lost in trying to comply with the current code.

IMPOSSIBLY COMPLEX

Today's tax code is so complex that many Americans despair that only someone with an advanced degree in rocket science could figure it out. They are wrong. Even a certified genius such as Albert Einstein needed help in figuring out his Form 1040.

Consider this example from the Internal Revenue Code's rules on the Earned Income Tax Credit. Here's how they describe the little human creature we call a child:

A IN GENERAL—The term "qualifying child" means, with respect to any taxpayer for any taxable year, an individual—

i who bears a relationship to the taxpayer described in subparagraph (B),

ii except as provided in subparagraph (B)(iii), who has the same principal place of abode as the taxpayer for more than one-half of such taxable year,

iii who meets the age requirements of subparagraph (C), and

iv with respect to whom the taxpayer meets the identification requirements of subparagraph (D).

This may look like English to the experts, but it is total gibberish to most other Americans. If nothing is done to simplify the impossible language of the current tax code, every American *will* need a laptop just to figure it out.

Professor James Eustice of NYU Law School once defined an "expert" as "a person who avoids small errors as he sweeps on to the grand fallacy." The problem with the tax code, he says, "is that it has been written and interpreted by so many 'experts' that it has lost sight of the fact that [real people] have to function under this system." The result is a tax code so complex that even the experts themselves can't figure it out. This was illustrated by an annual survey of tax experts conducted by *Money* magazine. Each year, the magazine would send a hypothetical tax return to fifty professional tax preparers, and every year it got back a startling range of responses, often encompassing 50 different answers. Needless to say, if the experts have trouble understanding the tax system, the odds are stacked against the rest of us.

Convoluted rules and regulations force small businesses to hire expensive accountants, forgo expansion or new opportunities, or in some cases avoid the entire mess by going underground. Tim Sabus of Denver, Colorado, wrote to the commission: "As an entrepreneur, I experience firsthand the horrors of our tax system. It has grown into a monstrous predator that kills incentives, swallows time, and chokes the hopes and dreams of many. We have abandoned several job-creating business concepts due to the tax complexities that would arise."

Another exasperated business owner, Frank Goodnight, told the commission at our Charlotte hearing that "during the recession of 1992, our company paid our accounting firm more money than we paid in taxes." He is not alone: In 1991, the Tax Foundation reported that small corporations spent a minimum of $382 in compliance costs for every $100 they paid in income taxes.

According to 1995 I.R.S. estimates, businesses will spend about 3.4 billion hours and individuals will spend about 1.7 billion hours embroiled in tax-related paperwork. That means nearly three million people—more people than serve in the U.S. armed forces—work full-time all year just to comply with tax laws, at a cost of about $200 billion a year, according to the Tax Foundation. In economic costs, this is like taking all the new cars, vans, and trucks that General Motors builds in a year and dumping them into the ocean.

In a recent hearing before the House Ways and Means Committee, William Dakin, senior tax counsel of Mobil, brought with him a huge stack of bound papers, weighing 76 pounds. These were Mobil's corporate tax forms for 1993. It cost Mobil an estimated $10 million, and the equivalent of 57 people working full-time for a year, just to figure how much tax the company owed. This is the essence of a brutally complicated tax system.

Jeff Renner, a real-estate developer from Bellevue, Nebraska, voiced the concern of many witnesses about the costly burden of compliance: "That time and effort and money did not educate a single child, it didn't feed a single family, and it didn't produce a single tangible object to improve the life of anyone." And Roger McCarthy who runs an engineering firm in Menlo Park, California, complained of how the tax industry absorbs the high-tech talent that could be working in productive fields: "It is disturbing that we are not competing with companies like Intel and Hewlett-Packard for these top stars, but rather with Big Six accounting firms."

OVERLY INTRUSIVE

There is no simple way of administering a monstrously complex tax code, just as there is no fair way of enforcing an unfair system. Former Treasury official Ernest S. Christian told the commission: "The present federal income tax code is a national disgrace that...has characteristics that would be condemned in any human personality. It is inexcusably class-conscious, it is hypocritical, it is meddlesome, it is overbearing, it is mean and hurtful, it is covetous, and above all, it is downright foolish." It is no wonder that the agency charged with enforcing such a system has become the object of increasing public ire.

Perhaps the most troublesome consequence of our modern-day income tax system is the enormous power that Congress has conferred on the Internal Revenue Service to force taxpayers to comply with the tax code. Twice as big as the C.I.A. and five times the size of the F.B.I., the I.R.S. controls more information about individual Americans than any other agency. Without a search warrant, the I.R.S. has the right to search the property and financial documents of American citizens. Without a trial, the I.R.S. has the right to seize property from Americans. What the I.R.S. calls its own "presumption of correctness" leaves many taxpayers feeling that they are "guilty until proven innocent"—a standard that turns norms of justice upside down.

Even those within the I.R.S. hierarchy concede the inquisitorial nature of the powers granted the agency. Fred Goldberg, former Commissioner of Internal Revenue, laments that "While it is unfair to the many fine people who work there, the I.R.S. has become a symbol of the most intrusive, oppressive, and non-democratic institution in our democratic society."

The code is so complicated that the I.R.S. itself has trouble understanding it. "As a retired revenue agent, I feel qualified to attest to the monstrosity that the Internal Revenue Code has become," a citizen from Michigan wrote to the commission. "When people who are employed to enforce the tax laws have difficulty understanding its complicated and sometimes incomprehensible provisions, it's time for a change." A General Accounting Office study found 16,000 errors in the liens filed by the I.R.S. in 1990. The error rate for penalty notices to employers on tax deposits has stood as high as 44 percent.

Even when the I.R.S. is not in error, many of its practices make little sense. For example, tax documents are not treated as "timely filed" if sent by Federal Express rather than the U.S. Postal Service. The I.R.S. charges taxpayers interest even when the taxpayer is due a refund. In another example, one particularly exasperated citizen wrote to the commission and enclosed a notice just received from the I.R.S. assessing a penalty against his company. For an underpayment of one cent on his tax returns, the company received a letter from the I.R.S. imposing a penalty of more than $150. Others should be so lucky. Many who testified before the commission told tales not just of tax penalties, but of thousands of dollars in legal fees and countless hours with lawyers in efforts to rectify minor and unwitting infractions, or clear their records of unjust charges.

In Charlotte, business owner Jean Hodges recounted a tale of horror in which she was forced to pay tens of thousands of dollars and spend untold hours trying to correct an error made by her company's bookkeeper. "I would like to see Congress pass legislation affording small businesses relief from onerous and intimidating I.R.S. regulations," she said.

The preceding pages illustrate what is wrong with the current tax system. But the case for a twenty-first-century tax system must be made by more than a mere indictment of the status quo. To paraphrase Peter Drucker: You have to decide what's right before you decide what's possible. The following chapter outlines principles upon which a better future can be built.

WORKING PRINCIPLES...FOR THE WAY AMERICA WORKS

When a group of architects sits down to design a new building, they don't start by picking out the draperies and choosing the color of the carpet. They begin by creating the basic outlines for the structure to come. Similarly, the charge and purpose of this commission is not to dictate the finishing touches of finalized legislation. Instead, it is to establish the foundation upon which a new system can be raised.

The commission's six working principles for a twenty-first-century tax system are not isolated ideas, randomly grouped, but rather principles that link together to form a sequence—a chain of economic DNA—that can renew the health of our economy and release the potential of the American people.

ECONOMIC GROWTH, the engine of opportunity and prosperity, can only be unleashed by a tax code that encourages initiative, hard work, and saving.

Such a system must be based on **FAIRNESS**, treating all citizens equally.

The system should achieve **SIMPLICITY**, so that anyone can figure it out.

A fair tax system also requires **NEUTRALITY**, because the tax code should not pick winners or losers, or tax saving more heavily than consumption.

The new tax system also needs **VISIBILITY**, so that everyone gets an honest accounting of government's cost.

A visible tax system will have **STABILITY**, so that people can plan for their futures.

ECONOMIC GROWTH

...Because expanding opportunity, prosperity, and social mobility form the foundation of a free and healthy society.
None of the myriad challenges confronting our nation—be they poverty, crime, racial tension, welfare dependence, or the budget deficit—can be solved without strong economic growth. Therefore, any new tax system must be predicated, first and foremost, on a commitment to revitalizing the American economy and lifting barriers to opportunity.

SHARE OF TAXES PAID BY THE TOP 1% INCREASED AS THE TOP RATE FELL

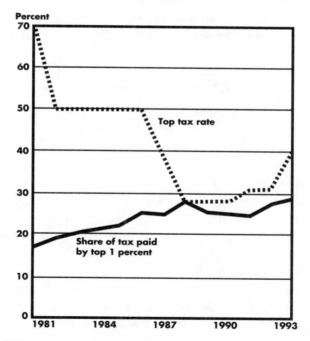

Source: IRS
There is an inverse relationship between revenue collections from the wealthy and high marginal tax rates.

TOP TAX RATE AND TOTAL FEDERAL REVENUES

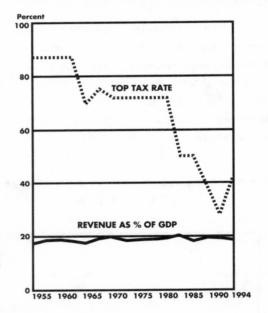

Source: IRS, OMB, Tax Foundation
The top line represents the top personal tax rates from 1952 to 1995. The bottom line shows revenue to the federal government expressed as a percentage of total economic output.

No nation has ever taxed its way to prosperity. Indeed, one of the world's fastest growing economies over the past 20 years, Hong Kong, has one of the lowest marginal tax rate systems—15 percent or less—on labor and capital. Throughout the ages, higher taxes have been inversely related to higher productivity and higher growth. Our own history provides evidence of this axiom.

America has experienced three periods of very strong economic growth in this century: the 1920s, the 1960s, and the 1980s. Each of these growth spurts coincided with a period of reductions in marginal tax rates. In the eight years following the first of the Harding–Coolidge tax cuts, the American economy grew by more than 5 percent per year. Following the Kennedy tax cuts in the early 1960s, the economy grew by nearly 5 percent per year and real tax revenues rose by 29 percent from 1962 to 1968 (after having remained flat for a decade). In the seven years following the 1981 Reagan tax cuts, the economy grew by nearly 4 percent per year while real federal revenues rose by 26 percent.

Over the years, we have seen economic output rise as tax rates fell (and fall as tax rates rose). But federal revenue raised as a percentage of national output has remained flat. As the accompanying graph on page 18 indicates, the federal government historically collects about 19 percent of gross domestic product—regardless of how high the tax rate has been pushed.

High rates simply mean a smaller economy—and less income to tax. Clearly, 19 percent of a small economy brings in less revenue than 19 percent of a big economy—one more reason why economic growth should be the goal of any new tax system. **This may be the most important point of the entire tax reform debate.**

FAIRNESS

...Because democracy is based on the principle of equality before the law.

One of the main themes the commission heard in hearings around the country is that taxpayers are willing to shoulder their share of the burden, as long as others pull their own weight as well. The current tax code—with its confusion of proliferating rates, deductions, exemptions, and transfers of wealth from one constituency to another—contributes to the overwhelming conviction of many Americans that the present system is unfair.

The definition of fairness that emerged from hours of testimony before the commission was clear and unambiguous. Any new system must satisfy three simple goals:

1. Tax equally: Does it treat taxpayers equally?

2.. True progressivity: Is it compassionate to those least able to pay?

3. Lower tax rates: Does it keep the tax rate low?

TAX EQUALLY

To most Americans, fairness means that the rules apply to everybody and everybody plays by the rules. Christine Perkowski of Richboro, Pennsylvania, wrote to the commission: "I do not mind paying my fair share as long as everyone else does, but I feel that many, many people and companies are not paying their fair share because they have the money to hire smart accountants and lawyers."

Under a simpler, fairer system, no one will get out of paying his or her share—no matter how many "smart accountants and lawyers" they can afford to hire. By streamlining the current Rube Goldberg contraption of multiple rates and rules, we can reduce the number of movable parts that are manipulated by those who seek to take advantage of the system.

Clearly, under the current multiple-rate system, any tax "loopholes"—deductions, exemptions, and credits—are more valuable to the wealthy than to those in lower brackets, reinforcing the perception that the rich do not pay their fair share. A single-rate system would level the playing field by eliminating the current distortion in which tax breaks are worth more when a person's income is higher.

On the other hand, while a single-rate system keeps pace with the taxpayer as he climbs the hill of economic opportunity, it does not weigh him down more heavily with higher rates at every step he tries to take. It addresses the issue raised by taxpayer Melvin Barlow of Las Cruces, New Mexico, who wrote to the commission: "It is not right that the harder a man works, the more he is taxed."

For taxable income above the personal exemption, if one taxpayer earns ten times as much as his neighbor, he should pay ten times as much in taxes. Not twenty times as much—as he would with multiple and confiscatory tax rates. Not five times as much—as he might with special loopholes. Ten times as much income, ten times as much taxes: That's the deal.

TRUE TAX PROGRESSIVITY

Americans must first be able to feed, clothe, and house their families before they are asked to feed the federal spending machine. A generous personal exemption will allow those citizens at the bottom of the economic ladder to gain a foothold and begin their climb before taxes take effect.

Today, those who try to move from welfare to work face the highest marginal tax rates in America. Some face effective tax rates higher than 100 percent, counting benefits that are lost, taxes that must now be paid, and costs associated with working. For example, if a single mother on welfare takes a job, her first paycheck may be more than canceled out by the economic hits she takes when she loses Aid to Families with Dependent Children, Medicaid, Food Stamps, and public housing allowances. In addition to losing benefits, she also must now pay Social Security and Medicare taxes, federal and probably state income tax, while facing a host of work-related costs, including transportation and child care. That means she stands to lose more than a dollar for every dollar she earns.

We need a tax system that expands opportunity and furthers economic independence by strengthening the link between effort and reward, not by slapping poverty-inducing tax rates on people as soon as they get their heads above water. True progressivity can be achieved by a single tax rate with a generous personal exemption. With an exemption, a "single rate" does not mean that everyone pays the same percentage of income in taxes. A generous personal exemption would remove the burden on those least able to pay. As incomes rise, the average tax rate gradually rises up to the single rate.

LOWER TAX RATES

The consensus of the majority of witnesses who wrote to the commission can be summed up in two words: **lower taxes.**

Historians may point to America's beginnings and a revolution deeply rooted in reaction to taxation of the original thirteen British colonies. Others reference religious traditions, including Moses' warning to Pharaoh that he may tax up to one fifth and no more—before demanding that he "let my people go." Indeed, Commissioner Dean Kleckner of Iowa touched a chord with many when he observed, half-jokingly, that "The Bible says we ought to tithe and give 10 percent to the Lord. I have a hard time with the concept of giving more to government than we're asked to give to God."

We suspect that most taxpayers have reached their conviction that taxes are too high not by consulting their history books or the Scriptures, but simply by comparing their weekly paychecks to their family budgets and counting all the sacrifices they must make simply to pay the government. While any new tax code must raise sufficient revenue to run the government, it must also be mindful of the burdens these taxes place on America's working families. One way to reduce this burden would be to restrain government spending. By restoring the balance of power between the federal government and the citizens who pay its bills, we can restore basic faith in the system and keep the tax rate low.

SIMPLICITY

...Because life is too short and peace of mind too precious to waste your time and lose your temper trying to figure out your taxes.

Filing tax returns will never be anyone's favorite pastime, but neither should it be what it has become: one of life's most nerve-wracking, gut-wrenching, and mind-numbing chores. With a simpler system, taxpayers will be able to file their returns on a single piece of paper in less time than it takes to finish the morning crossword puzzle.

As detailed earlier, the current tax code is exceedingly expensive to comply with, increasingly difficult to enforce, and nearly impossible to understand. Ambiguities and inconsistencies in the current tax code increase the likelihood that taxpayers will make mistakes and fall victim to enforcement techniques considered by many to be infringements of personal liberties.

Long ago the authors of the *Federalist Papers* warned, "It will be of little avail to the people that the laws are made by men of their own choice if the laws be so voluminous that they cannot be read, or so incoherent that they cannot be understood." A simplified, fairer tax system will let Americans get a handle on their taxes, a grip on their government, and a hold on their future.

NEUTRALITY

...Because the tax code should not pick winners or play favorites, but allow people freely to make decisions based on their own needs and dreams.

The tax code should be used to raise revenue to run the government while doing the least possible damage to the economy. This means leaving individuals free to make decisions and to set priorities based on economic reality—not on the bureaucratic whims of Washington, D.C.

Taxes cannot help but raise the cost of everything they fall on. But at least they should fall on things neutrally without penalizing one form of economic behavior and promoting another. As Senator Robert Bennett of Utah recently pointed out, "Neutrality means that the tax code should not be used to punish the bad guys and reward the good guys. We have other laws for that." Unfortunately, the current code strives to act as economic traffic cop—giving green lights to certain economic activities and red lights to others.

The result of the biases and distortions in the current system is to make the market less free, the system less fair, and families less financially secure. As Frank Hayes, a public accountant who testified before the commission in Omaha, remarked: "If there's a way to make things simpler and take the tax aspect out of making day-to-day decisions, I think everybody would become productive."

Perhaps the single most irrational and economically damaging aspect of today's code is the layer upon layer of taxes on saving and investment. By hitting income saved and invested harder and more frequently than income consumed, the current system prompts taxpayers to spend today what they might otherwise save for tomorrow. This is particularly alarming considering the problems facing public retirement programs and the need to strengthen private retirement saving. The Bipartisan Commission on Entitlement and Tax Reform has offered useful analyses and proposals on this subject.

VISIBILITY

...Because those who pay the price of government have a right to see the bill.

The history of hidden taxes, rapidly rising rates, and perpetual budget deficits proves that what you don't know can hurt you. The current system hides the cost of government behind a chronic deficit and a maddening multiplicity of taxes—many of which are virtually invisible to the taxpayer who pays them. How much did we pay in payroll taxes last year? What excise taxes were hidden in the prices of the products we bought? What are the tax costs of exclusions, deductions, and corporate income taxes? Most of us answer these questions with a shrug.

When it comes to these hidden levies, ignorance is expensive bliss indeed.

One of the biggest political fictions in American history is the progressive taxation of "Mr. Nobody"—the illusion that "painless" taxes can be levied on businesses and on the goods and services they sell. But goods and services do not pay taxes. People do. While businesses collect taxes, the burden of paying the "business" taxes ultimately falls on each one of us as investors, workers, or consumers.

Moreover, the invisibility of many taxes perpetuates the fantasy that government is free—even as its real costs shrink our paychecks, sap our savings, drain our economy, and inflate the budget deficit to ominous proportions. Bob Genetski, an economist and author who testified at hearings in Omaha, told the commission: "The cost of government is not obvious to people. If you hide the cost of government, people are going to demand more government than they otherwise would." By severing the connection between government's cost and its consumption, the current system deprives citizens of the information they need in order to make rational choices about what they want to buy from Washington and how much they are willing to spend.

A visible system gives taxpayers an honest accounting of government's expense and will make it far more difficult for politicians to tinker with the tax code without democratic consent. The incurable cynic H. L. Mencken once said, "Conscience is the inner voice which warns us somebody may be looking." By making taxes visible, we can ensure that someone always will be.

STABILITY

...Because taxpayers should be able to plan for their future without the rules being changed in the middle of the game.

Everyone has heard the old saw that there are only two things in life that are certain: death and taxes. Given the constant changes to the tax code over the past few decades, the certainty of taxes has taken a perverse twist. Like walking blindfolded down a ship's gangplank, you know the end is out there—you just don't know when it will arrive, how far you will fall, or how long you will be able to keep your head above water.

This uncertainty has a debilitating effect on the economy, making it very difficult for families and businesses, particularly small businesses, to plan for their future with confidence. This exacts a tremendous cost from those taxpayers and business owners who must struggle to keep up with ever-shifting rules and regulations. The retroactive tax increases passed in 1993 packed a double whammy—changing the rules when the game was half over. A stable tax code must allow individuals to start a business, buy a house, take out a loan, put money into savings, or plan for their children's education without fear of what might lurk behind the next election cycle.

We know what works: Freedom works. And only principles for tax reform that maximize freedom can yield the opportunities, economic growth, and untold possibilities for human advancement that are its fruits. In his last public address, Abraham Lincoln declared that "Important principles may and must be inflexible." By laying down these important principles, this commission hopes to help build a future of growing prosperity for many generations to come.

A NEW TAX SYSTEM FOR THE
TWENTY-FIRST CENTURY

RECOMMENDATIONS

Among the hundreds of testimonies and citizen letters reviewed by this commission, one of the most compelling was that of Van Woods, owner of Sylvia's Restaurant. Mr. Woods and his family run a successful soul food establishment in the heart of Harlem, a community with painfully high unemployment. In concluding his testimony to the commission, he said, "Opportunity is the ability to look in the face of my son and say: 'I don't know if you *will* succeed, but you *can*.' "

The objective of this commission, the aim of its members, is to help make that promise a reality—not just for Van Woods's children but for every child in every neighborhood in America's twenty-first century.

In submitting these recommendations, the commission does not seek to toss yet another piece of legislation on the table. Nor was our goal to pick and choose among existing plans, or worse, create a hodgepodge compromise from elements of existing alternatives. What we are offering to the American people and their elected officials is a set of standards—a quality control—that any new plan must meet if it is to achieve the bold objective of replacing the current tax code with a fair and simple system. The preceding chapter provides one half of the checklist: the principles that any new system should embody.

- **Economic growth** through incentives to work, save, and invest

- **Fairness** for all taxpayers

- **Simplicity**, so that everyone can figure it out

- **Neutrality**, so that people and not government can make choices

- **Visibility**, so that people know the cost of government

- **Stability**, so that people can plan for their future

This chapter provides the other half of the tax test: key recommendations that any new system should follow.

The core recommendations of the National Commission on Economic Growth and Tax Reform are:

- **Adopt a single, low tax rate with a generous personal exemption.**

- **Lower the tax burden on America's working families and remove it on those least able to pay.**

- **End biases against work, saving, and investing.**

- **Allow full deductibility of the payroll tax for working men and women.**

- **Require a two-thirds super-majority vote in Congress to increase tax rates.**

We believe that, with a pro-growth, pro-family tax system, we can achieve these goals and satisfy these principles within the context of budget equilibrium.

The following pages explain these core recommendations and explore some of the trade-offs involved in reaching a system that meets these goals. This chapter also touches on a few of the corollary points that flow from these main recommendations. Staff discussion papers are provided beginning on page 43 for those who seek more detail on the concepts involved.

RECOMMENDATIONS

Single tax rate.

A single rate is fair. One tax rate, coupled with a generous personal exemption, together produce a progressive average tax rate. Low-income taxpayers would owe little or no tax. But everyone who earns enough to cross the threshold of the exemption would face exactly the same tax rate on any additional income.

A single-rate system is not only fair, it also can satisfy the principles of simplicity, visibility, and stability. A single rate is clearly simple, and it is highly visible: one rate—as opposed to the current, confusing mess—will stand out and be remembered by all. A simple, visible system also can be stable: By keeping our eyes on the single rate, we can keep politicians' hands off it.

Nobel Prize–winning economist F. A. Hayek described economic redistribution through multiple tax rates as "the chief source of irresponsibility" in politics and "the crucial issue on which the whole character of future society will depend." A system of graduated marginal rates violates the principle of fairness—that if a law applies to citizen A, it must equally apply to citizen B.

Take, for example, two wheat producers, each farming the same-sized plot of land. One of them produces 1,000 bushels of wheat; the other, through harder work and more careful land management, produces 1,200 bushels. To tax the income represented by the additional 200 bushels of wheat more heavily than the income represented by the first 1,000 would be demonstrably unfair to the more productive farmer. And yet, that is the nature of a multi-rate tax system: It takes more from people for their hard work, creativity, and success.

The added output—and the resulting added income—of one taxpayer does not diminish his neighbor, and is not earned at his neighbor's expense. Indeed, it expands economic opportunity, increases the availability of goods and services, and helps others be more productive as well.

True progressivity requires a low tax rate coupled with a generous

BIAS AGAINST SAVING AND INVESTMENT34

Multiple taxation creates a huge bias against saving and investment that must be eliminated in a new system. Consider, for example, the effect of the current system on a family in the 28 percent tax bracket that earns an extra $1,000.

Of that $1,000, they will pay $280 in federal income tax and keep $720. If they spend that $720, say, taking the family to Disneyland, they incur no further federal tax, no matter how many times they ride the Space Mountain.

But suppose, instead, they decide to invest the income in stocks to create financial security for their future. Bad move, says the current tax code.

First, they already had to pay income taxes to have the $720 to invest. Second, the company in which they invest will generally pay tax at a 35 percent rate on the returns on the amount invested. Third, if the company pays dividends, the family will pay a 28 percent tax on the dividends they receive. Alternatively, if the company retains the after-tax income for reinvestment or finds other ways to boost future earnings, the stock price will rise. The future earnings will be taxed, and if the family sells the stock, it will pay a capital gains tax at a 28 percent rate. Fourth, if they hold the proceeds of the sale until death, they will be subject to an estate tax that can go as high as 55 percent. State and local taxes add to these burdens.

Both the investment in the stock market and the investment in the family trip produce returns—one yields warm memories of the past, the other provides real hope for the future. The returns on the investment in the trip are not subject to tax; the returns on the investment in the stock market are.

personal exemption. This would grant low-income Americans an "economic headstart"—allowing them to begin their climb toward economic independence before they are asked to shoulder their share of government's cost. The larger goal is to move beyond merely maintaining low-income Americans at subsistence-level livelihoods toward giving them an opportunity to permanently escape poverty.

Here, as elsewhere, there are trade-offs involved. The goal of protecting those least able to bear the burden of taxation conflicts with the principle of visibility: Those exempt from taxes don't see the price of the government services we all pay for. The commission believes that the costs—both economic and moral—of burdening low-income people with taxes that can bar them from reaching their fullest potential outweigh competing concerns. By offering low-income Americans a window of economic opportunity, the personal exemption can help liberate those whom the public sector has failed to help and the private sector has failed to reach.

Lower Tax Rates.

The commission recommends that the single rate be as low as possible. We encourage the adoption of such a low rate within the framework of budget equilibrium. Furthermore, we strongly urge that the rate be lowered over time as a growing economy yields rising revenues. We recommend that added revenues be considered, not as more Monopoly money for Washington, but as a "growth dividend" to be paid out to the American people.

Eliminate Biases Against Work, Saving, and Investment.

The principles of fairness and neutrality require that all income be taxed the same, whether it is used for consumption or saving, whether it is produced in small businesses or large corporations, and whether it is earned by employees or the self-employed.

Under the current system, income that is used for consumption is taxed once, while income that is saved is taxed again and again. For businesses, complex depreciation rules mean that income from investment in buildings and equipment is overstated. This forces people to pay taxes before they have recovered the cost of their investment.

The box on page 30 provides examples of the problems created by the current tax code.

The biases result in less work, saving, and investment, lower productivity and wages, fewer jobs, less income to spend on housing and education, and fewer assets to provide income in retirement than would otherwise be the case. As these examples demonstrate, these biases affect every family that is trying to save for the future.

To end these biases, **the tax system must 1) either let savers deduct their saving or exclude the returns on the saving from their taxable income; 2) end double taxation of businesses and their owners; and 3) permit expensing of investment outlays.** (See discussion papers.) It must also address the following issues:

Capital Gains Taxes.

If a new tax system is to eliminate biases against saving and investment, it also must abolish separate taxation of capital gains. As commissioner Ted Forstmann said, "The biggest depressant on the rate of capital formation is the risk of confiscation by the government." The United States now imposes some of the highest tax rates on capital of any developed nation—a 28 percent tax on long-term capital gains unindexed for inflation. Compare that with a 16 percent rate in France; a 1 percent rate in Japan; and a zero tax on capital gains in Hong Kong, Germany, South Korea, Singapore, and Malaysia.

The result is to punish risk-taking, shrink the pool of capital needed for investment, and deprive would-be entrepreneurs of a chance to climb the ladder of economic opportunity. "The tax on capital gains," argued President Kennedy in 1963, "directly affects investment decisions, the mobility and the flow of risk capital...the ease or difficulty experienced by new ventures in obtaining capital, and thereby the strength and potential for growth in the economy."

By shrinking the supply of available seed corn, the capital gains tax acts as a future tax on wealth to be realized, businesses to be built, and jobs to be created. Those hardest hit are not the wealthy—who by definition have their capital gains, their wealth, behind them—but rather all those who have yet to realize their capital gains: the poor, the young, and minorities.

"Death" Taxes.

It makes little sense and is patently unfair to impose extra taxes on people who choose to pass their assets on to their children and grandchildren instead of spending them lavishly on themselves. Families faced with these confiscatory taxes often find themselves forced to sell off farms or businesses, destroying jobs in the process. "We must help to save the family farm, ranch, and business," said Commissioner Jack Faris.

Unfortunately, family businesses often get hit hardest because they can't afford to hire expensive lawyers and accountants. As Douglas Darch of Wake Forest, North Carolina, testified to the commission: "There is something wrong with a tax system that results in the systematic dismantling of small businesses to meet estate tax obligations."

The tragedy is that while these taxes cause much suffering for tax-paying families, they generate relatively little revenue. Estate and gift taxes count for less than 1 percent of federal revenues—but even that low figure is exaggerated and misleading. Professor Douglas Bernheim of Stanford University testified before the commission that the estate tax may not really raise any revenue at all, because more income tax is lost from "estate planning" than is ultimately collected at death.

Full Deductibility of Payroll Taxes for All Working Americans.

The commission recommends that federal payroll taxes be fully deductible—both for employers and employees. Many employers and employees pay more in payroll taxes than they do in federal income taxes. Making these taxes deductible for both employers and employees will reduce obstacles to hiring more workers and will fuel America's job growth into the twenty-first century.

Under the current tax system, workers pay income tax on their Social Security tax—a tax on a tax. Employers can deduct their half of the payroll tax, but employees cannot. The combined burden of both income and Social Security tax is particularly hard on workers with incomes too high to be eligible for the Earned Income Tax Credit (roughly $25,000), but too low to be below the threshold where the Social Security tax stops being taken out of paychecks (about $63,000).

When employer and employee payroll taxes of 15.3 percent are taken into account, workers in the 28 percent tax bracket actually face a brutal marginal tax rate of more than 43 percent on any additional income they earn. A single, low tax rate would help relieve this demoralizing tax penalty on work and saving. But it still leaves a tax on a tax.

Making the Social Security tax deductible would help reduce the combined marginal tax rates on middle-income taxpayers who get hit by both taxes. A one-earner couple with a $40,000 income currently pays tax as though the couple really received the entire $40,000—even though they have already paid over $3,000 as their share of the payroll tax, leaving less than $37,000 on which they could possibly pay income taxes. By making the payroll tax deductible, income taxes would be calculated on the basis of working families' real net incomes.

The need for change was highlighted in a citizen letter to the commission from Spencer Riedel of Flagstaff, Arizona, who described the Social Security payroll tax as "a huge heartache," asking: "Is there no way to stop this 'hidden' tax?... If we could eliminate this unfair mandated tax, our business would hire two more people."

A Two-Thirds Majority Vote in Congress to Raise the Tax Rate.

The commission recommends that the new system be guaranteed by requiring a super-majority vote of both houses of Congress to raise the rate.

In hearings across the country, one depressing but all-too-familiar response from taxpayers could be bluntly paraphrased as: "Change, schmange. That's what you guys said the last time you talked about tax reform." The roller-coaster ride of tax policy in the past few decades has fed citizens' cynicism about the possibility of real, long-term reform, while fueling frustration with Washington. The initial optimism inspired by the low rates of the 1986 Tax Reform Act soured into disillusionment and anger when taxes subsequently were hiked two times in less than seven years. The commission believes that a two-thirds super-majority vote of Congress will earn Americans' confidence in the longevity and stability of any new tax system.

The goal: A single, low rate on income with a generous personal exemption, a lower burden on working families, an end to biases in the tax code—all set in the stone of a congressional super-majority. The recommendations in this chapter form the core framework for a new twenty-first-century tax system.

OTHER ISSUES

Deductions and Exclusions.

Concerns about special provisions in the existing tax code have the potential to derail debate over the merits of a new tax system and the tremendous expansion and opportunities it could bring to the American economy. We recognize that there are important social and economic consequences of certain deductions and exclusions. The commission believes they should be considered with an eye to their impact on the tax rate, the costs to the Treasury, the consequences of change—and with respect to the values of the American people. For example, the home mortgage interest deduction has strengthened home ownership in America. And our commission supports the need to spread ownership so that more people have a stake in the system. In addition, at a time when America needs a renaissance of private giving and commitment to overcome those social problems that government programs have either failed to improve or made worse, we need a system that encourages people to take more responsibility for their communities and neighbors in need. We welcome debate over the best way to protect these institutions and preserve the values they represent within the context of the dynamic new tax system we envision.

Simplify International Taxation.

Congress should consider a territorial tax system. The current system of taxing international business operations is one of the most complicated parts of the Internal Revenue Code. It leads to enormous costs of compliance and enforcement, raises little revenue, and damages American competitiveness abroad. Further, it encourages U.S. businesses to keep reinvesting profits abroad rather than bringing the money back home where it could be reinvested in America.

Whatever new tax system is chosen, there must be a clearer, simpler, and more certain determination, relative to current practice, of what income is foreign or domestic or what international transaction is taxable. In addition, attention must be given to the proper tax treatment of foreign source license fees, royalties, and other intangibles so as not to discourage research and development in the United States.

Strengthen Private Retirement Saving.

The commission is particularly concerned that Americans are not saving enough for their own retirement. A tax system that eliminates the bias against saving is essential to encourage people to accumulate more assets throughout their lives. There is, however, no guarantee that all individuals or families will save enough to be secure and financially independent in their retirement, even under a new tax system.

With the problems facing public retirement programs, it is essential that private retirement saving be strengthened. Without sufficient retirement saving, many people will become dependent upon the government in their old age, necessitating either sharp increases in taxes on future generations or a significantly diminished standard of living. Providing strong encouragement for individuals and families to take responsibility for their own retirement will go a long way toward preventing uncontrolled growth of government while ensuring a more comfortable, more secure, and more independent retirement.

Therefore, any tax system should encourage people to save for their own retirement. The commission recommends that Congress adopt changes that will result in people taking more responsibility for their own retirement saving. The first step is to end the bias against saving. Other changes within the overall income and payroll tax systems also should be considered.

MEASURING RESULTS

One cannot catch the blossoming of a rose in a split-second single-frame exposure, or capture a speeding bullet with time-lapse photography. Similarly, the tools with which we anticipate and examine changes in government policies, including tax policy, must mirror the way the economy actually changes as a result of these actions.

The most important consequence of an unbiased, single-rate system will be an expansion of the economy. Expanded revenues from an expanding economy will offset a large portion of the "costs" to the Treasury of lower tax rates on work, saving, and investment. Failure to count these added revenues presents a skewed picture of the economic consequences of a new, simplified tax system—and makes reform appear more costly to the Treasury than it actually is.

When a bill is being debated before Congress, members are required to produce estimates of the costs of the legislation. For years, Congress has used what are called "static revenue estimates" to produce these figures. Static revenue estimates attempt to predict future government revenues by applying the new law to today's economy as though it would not be affected by the new law. History has shown that these estimates are limited in their ability to predict revenues.

We recommend that Congress instead use estimates that measure the impact policy changes will have on people's behavior and on future economic activity, and that therefore more accurately predict implications for future revenue collections. Use of this "dynamic" scoring, of course, must be based upon realistic assumptions regarding tax rates, tax revenues, and economic activity. It is essential to avoid overly optimistic as well as overly pessimistic projections. (Further details are provided in the staff discussion papers.)

TRANSITION ISSUES

The recommendations outlined here can lay the groundwork for a pro-growth, pro-family tax code for America's twenty-first century. As construction of the new system moves forward, there will be many decisions to be met and made along the way. While we have tried to raise a number of those issues here, and clarify others in the discussion papers, it is impossible to anticipate every question that will arise as we move toward a new system.

We urge that the American people participate in this debate at every step of the way. This is all the more crucial given the critical nature of the transition issues involved as replacement of the current system gets underway. Half a century ago, the economist Joseph Schumpeter described capitalism as inseparable from "the perennial gale of creative destruction." In the transition to a fairer system and a freer market, the winds of change are bound to increase. Those who have a stake in the status quo will not welcome change; others may prefer the cramped confines of the familiar present to the uncertainty of a yet to be realized future.

We know the naysayers will try to claim that our recommendations will mean a tax increase on the middle class or cause a flood of red ink.

These claims play on fear—but are not grounded in fact. The arguments advanced to defend the current system are trapped in the same mentality which helped create it—the impulse to try and squeeze more revenue through higher taxes and divide Americans along class lines. Emerson once said that "The field cannot well be seen from within the field." Status-quo thinkers are so bent on preserving the present system that they have blinded themselves to the brilliant rainbow of new benefits a new system would bring—from more jobs, to higher wages, to lower interest rates, to greater compliance. These rewards will help ease transition, and help pay for the changes involved.

That doesn't mean there won't be challenging issues to address as we move towards a new system. In particular, policy makers must take care to protect existing savings, investments, and other assets. Whatever the challenges this change presents, we believe that none of the issues is insurmountable.

CONCLUSION

If the taxpayer testimonies we listened to and letters we received bear any evidence of the broader mood of the country, Americans are impatient for change, ready for its challenges, and eager for its opportunities.

It has been a privilege for each of us on this commission to serve the American people in bringing that change closer to realization. We have been educated and inspired by the many taxpayers we have heard from around the country. While the tax system is in serious disrepair, the American spirit and optimism are stronger than ever. We thank Senate Majority Leader Dole and Speaker Gingrich for giving us this opportunity by appointing us to do this important work.

We quote in this report many of the citizen witnesses who wrote to us and who testified at our hearing. We thank them and the many expert witnesses who prepared testimony and answered our many questions about the intricacies of tax reform.

We are very much indebted to the lawmakers who have spent years of their careers studying tax reform, inspiring serious debate on the flaws of the current system, and developing proposals for major reform. Among them: House Majority Leader Dick Armey, Ways and Means Chairman Bill Archer, Senate Budget Chairman Pete Domenici, Senator Sam Nunn, Joint Economic Committee Chairman Connie Mack, Senator Bob Bennett, and Congressman Dick Gephardt. Others whose work has been invaluable to the process include Senator Richard Shelby, Senator Richard Lugar, Senator Arlen Specter, ranking Ways and Means Committee member Sam Gibbons, and many others.

It has been said that every breakthrough in human understanding has come in the form of a simplification. The complex, bureaucratic tax code of the twentieth century will not enable us to keep pace with the complex and rapidly changing world of the twenty-first century. A simplified tax code would have an instant impact on peoples' lives—freeing up time, energy, and resources currently wasted in costly compliance for productive endeavors.

The impact on the economy would be immediate and profound, putting the goal of a decade of doubled economic growth rate within our reach. The moment the dead weight and distortions of the current tax system are lifted from our economy, the explosion of new investment, new businesses, and new jobs would transform the economic and social landscape of our country. A newly galvanized economy would create work for all those who wanted it, unleash unimagined innovations, act as a magnet for capital from all over the world, and boost wages and living standards for America's working families.

We also believe that a new tax code can help replenish the wellsprings of public trust—in our government, in each other, and in ourselves. By treating citizens equally and with respect, a new tax code can restore faith in the basic fairness of the system. A simplified system will eliminate the fear that special advantages hide in complexity, while restoring citizens' confidence in their own ability to comply with the code.

This vision of the future is rooted in both a realism about human nature and an idealism about human potential. We recognize that a new tax code, no matter how radical, cannot solve all problems. It cannot make fathers love mothers or guarantee children happy homes. Government reform, however vast or vaunted, cannot change hearts.

But it can lift hopes. At its best, it does this by seeking, as Lincoln did, "to elevate the condition of men—lift artificial weights from all shoulders—to clear the paths of laudable pursuit for all."

By freeing citizens from the costly encumbrances of the current tax code, by restoring the link between effort and reward, by allowing individuals to save and invest in their future, and by unleashing the pent-up power of our economy, this new system can lead to Lincoln's "new birth of freedom," and launch us into the next American century.

THE TAX TEST

SIX POINTS OF PRINCIPLE

❑ Economic growth through incentives to work, save, and invest.

❑ Fairness for all taxpayers.

❑ Simplicity, so everyone can figure it out.

❑ Neutrality, so people and not government make choices.

❑ Visibility, so people know the cost of government.

❑ Stability, so people can plan for the future.

SIX POINTS OF POLICY

❑ A single tax rate.

❑ A generous personal exemption to remove the burden on those least able to pay.

❑ Lower tax rates for America's families.

❑ Payroll tax deductibility for workers.

❑ Ending biases against work, saving, and investing.

❑ Making the new tax system hard to change.

PART TWO
DISCUSSION AND
BACKGROUND PAPERS

The following briefing papers were prepared by commission staff and economic consultants to assist in the deliberations of the National Commission on Economic Growth and Tax Reform. These papers provide more detail on some of the concepts and issues that were considered by the commission. For more information, please contact the authors. Contact information is listed at the end of each paper.

Grace-Marie Arnett
Executive Director
Tax Reform Commission

Alan Reynolds
Research Director
Tax Reform Commission

CONSULTANTS:
Stephen J. Entin, **Institute for Research on the Economics of Taxation**
Daniel Mitchell, **Heritage Foundation**
Bruce Bartlett, **National Center for Policy Analysis**
Stephen Moore, **CATO Institute**

HISTORICAL LESSONS FOR TAX REFORM

Tax reform is not a voyage into uncharted waters. America has experienced many dramatic changes in income tax policy. These changes offer valuable lessons about the impact of tax policy and indicate that a single rate system will yield great benefits. The United States has had three major episodes of individual income tax rate reductions—the 1920s, 1960s, and 1980s. In all three periods, individual income tax revenues increased in general, and the amount of taxes paid by the rich rose in particular. All three periods, not coincidentally, saw strong economic growth.

Periods of rising tax rates, by contrast, are associated with weaker economic performance and slower revenue growth. Tax rate increases in the 1930s, starting with Herbert Hoover's decision to boost the top rate from 25 percent to 63 percent, contributed to the economy's misery during the depression years. Inflation-induced bracket creep in the 1970s and early 1980s certainly hindered economic growth in the 1973–1982 period (prior to the 1981 tax rate reductions and indexing). Finally, tax increases in the 1990s have resulted in sub-par growth and stagnant incomes.

As John F. Kennedy said, a growing economy is the best way to raise earnings and living standards.

LOOKING AT THE EVIDENCE: THE 1920S

The Revenue Acts of 1921, 1924, and 1926 slashed individual income tax rates and reduced the top rate from 73 percent to 25 percent.

Notwithstanding (or perhaps because of) the dramatic reduction in tax rates, individual income tax revenues increased substantially during the 1920s, rising from $719 million in 1921 to $1,160 million in 1928, an increase of more than 61 percent (with near zero inflation). The share of the tax burden paid by the rich (incomes over $50,000 in the 1920s) rose dramatically, climbing from 44.2 percent in 1921 to 78.4 percent in 1928.

Andrew Mellon, the Treasury Secretary who oversaw the tax cuts, wrote, "Taxes which are inherently excessive are not paid. The high rates inevitably put pressure upon the taxpayer to withdraw his capital from productive business and invest it in tax-exempt securities or to find other lawful methods of avoiding the realization of taxable income. The result is that the sources of taxation are drying up; wealth is failing to carry its share of the tax burden; and capital is being diverted into channels which yield neither revenue to the Government nor profit to the people."

LOOKING AT THE EVIDENCE: THE 1960S

President Kennedy proposed a series of individual income tax rate reductions in 1963 that resulted in legislation that dropped the top tax rate from 91 percent in 1963 to 70 percent by 1965. Income tax revenues grew strongly, climbing by more than 16 percent between 1963 and 1966. As happened during the 1920s, the share of the income tax burden borne by the rich increased. Tax collections from those making over $50,000 per year climbed by 57 percent between 1963 and 1966 while tax collections from those earning below $50,000 rose 11 percent. As a result, the "rich" saw their portion of the income tax burden climb from 11.6 percent to 15.1 percent.

LOOKING AT THE EVIDENCE: THE 1980S-1990S

President Reagan presided over two major pieces of tax legislation that together reduced the top individual income tax rate from 70 percent in 1980 to 28 percent by 1988. Earnings for all income groups rose during the 1980s once tax rate reductions went into effect. Beginning in January of 1983, income tax revenues climbed dramatically, increasing by more than 54 percent by 1989 (28 percent after adjusting for inflation). The share of income taxes paid by the top 10 percent of earners jumped significantly, climbing from 48.0 percent in 1981 to 57.2 percent in 1988. The top one percent saw their share of the income tax bill climb even more dramatically, from 17.6 percent in 1981 to 27.5 percent in 1988.

Tax rate increases in recent years, however, have resulted in a weaker economy. Ironically, even though tax rate increases in 1990 and 1993 were supposed to make the "rich" pay more, the rate increases have backfired. In 1991, income taxes paid by those earning more than $200,000 fell by 6.1 percent while income taxes paid by those with lower earnings rose by one percent. The adverse consequences of the 1990 tax increase are being matched by similar evidence from the 1993 tax increase. According to I.R.S data, taxable income among those with earnings of less than $200,000 climbed by 3.3 percent between 1992 and 1993. For those with earnings over $200,000, however, taxable income declined by 2.3 percent.

The deficit is higher today than it was when President Reagan left office. It may turn out that deficits are higher because tax increases caused revenues to fall. Consider this evidence: Individual income tax revenues totaled 8.6 percent of economic output in 1989. By 1994—two large tax increases later—individual income tax revenues had fallen to 8.2 percent of economic output.

It is said that those who forget history's mistakes are doomed to repeat them. Conversely, those who recognize the successes of the past will be better positioned to move the country forward in the future. The commission's report can point the way to build on the successes of previous improvements in tax policy.

For more information, contact:
Daniel Mitchell, The Heritage Foundation, 214 Massachusetts Ave., N.E., Washington, D.C. 20002. Phone: (202) 546-4400.

BENEFITS OF A SINGLE TAX RATE SYSTEM

The widespread recognition that high tax rates hinder economic growth has contributed to the growing support for tax reform. Does this mean, however, that a new tax system cannot have more than one rate? If low tax rates are important, then would not a tax code with rates of 10 percent and 20 percent be just as good as a flat tax of 15 percent? And would not a system with rates of 15 percent and 20 percent be better than a flat tax of 20 percent?

In fact, there are substantial benefits from a single-rate system in terms of fairness, stability, and simplicity, as the following discussion makes clear.

A Single Rate Defines Fairness:

At hearings across the country the commission heard one theme repeated over and over again. People do not want special privileges, but neither do they want special penalties. By an overwhelming margin, citizens want taxpayers to be treated equally. In the 14th Amendment, states are prohibited from denying persons within their jurisdiction "equal protection of the laws." The same principle should hold for the tax code. If one taxpayer has ten times as much taxable income as his neighbor, he should pay ten times as much in taxes. Not twenty times as much, which is what happens when a discriminatory rate structure is imposed. But neither should the taxpayer with ten times the income get away with paying only five times as much in taxes, which is what happens when the tax code is vulnerable to clever machinations by lawyers, lobbyists, and accountants.

A Single Rate Promotes Efficiency and Growth:

Taxing all potential producers of additional goods and services at the same tax rate gives everyone an equal incentive to add to the output of the economy. The current graduated rate system imposes higher tax rates the more one produces and discourages those who are most efficient. It particularly discourages people from taking risks and making innovations and investments that could lead to the greatest economic rewards not only for themselves but for workers and consumers as well.

A Single Rate Is Progressive:

All taxpayers should be able to protect some level of income from taxation. Whatever this amount is called—a zero-bracket amount, a family allowance, or a personal exemption—it represents an economic headstart that permits taxpayers to satisfy the basic requirements for food, clothing, and shelter before the tax collector demands a share. One result of this headstart is that it builds progressivity into the single-rate system. Low-income taxpayers would have a bigger share of their income exempted from taxes, and would enjoy a lower average tax rate, than higher-income taxpayers. Above the exempt amount, a single-rate tax would be proportional: A taxpayer with ten times the income of his neighbor would pay ten times as much in taxes.

A Single Rate Will Make It Harder for Future Politicians to Undo Tax Reform:

Witnesses expressed concern over and over again that the Congress not repeat the mistakes of the 1986 Tax Reform Act. That law, taxpayers complained, was supposed to reform the tax code by eliminating deductions and giving taxpayers lower rates, but by 1993 top tax rates had crept much of the way back up to the pre-1986 levels. One reason that the 1986 Act proved so unstable was that it never achieved a single rate. As a result, taxpayers were subject to the old divide-and-conquer game. Single-rate systems, by contrast, are much more stable. In 1994, for instance, Massachusetts voters were given an opportunity to replace the state's flat tax with a so-called progressive system. The voters of the state rejected the proposal by a landslide margin of 71 percent. They knew that once the state had the opportunity to tax one group at a higher rate, it would only be a matter of time before all taxpayers wound up paying more. If there were a single rate tax at the federal level, stability would be built into the system.

A Single Rate Eliminates the Marriage Penalty:
Under current law, the first dollar of income for a nonworking spouse who enters the labor market is taxed as if it were additional income for the primary earner. In a system of graduated rates, this means that incomes that normally would be subject to marginal tax rates of 15 percent are actually being taxed at rates of 28 percent or more. This policy undermines work incentives, reduces employment, and lowers tax revenues. Needless to say, it is also unfair to married couples with two incomes.

A Single Rate Avoids Tax Timing Problem:
Many taxpayers, including farmers and small business owners, have volatile incomes. In a single-rate system, they are not punished if their income is sharply higher in one year than another. In a system of discriminatory graduated tax rates, however, they suffer if their income is received unevenly. Under graduated rates, people who can do so have an incentive to engage in costly end-of-year exercises to ensure that income is reported in the tax year where it will be subject to lower rates. Just the opposite occurs with deductions. A small business owner may delay or hasten the purchase of some equipment depending on whether last year's, this year's, or next year's income is subject to a lower tax rate. All this complexity disappears with a single rate system.

Fairness, simplicity, and growth all require a new tax system that taxes income only once and does so at a low, single rate. The most profound argument for one rate, however, is trust. Tax reform represents a compact with the American people, one that taxpayers could be reluctant to embrace after what happened in 1986 and beyond. In order to ensure that a new tax system will not be undermined and destroyed by future politicians, it must be extremely hard to change. This, more than any other reason, is why one rate is so necessary.

For more information, contact:
Daniel Mitchell, The Heritage Foundation, 214 Massachusetts Ave.,
N.E., Washington, D.C. 20002. Phone: (202) 546-4400.

TAXES ON THE POOR

Some of the highest implicit tax rates fall on poor individuals as they try to work their way off welfare. Not only do they have to pay taxes on the income that they earn, but they also have their welfare benefits reduced. This reduction in benefits is a de facto tax, because it reduces their net income the same way direct taxes do.

Depending on the precise combination of earnings, taxes, and benefits, a welfare mother can easily face marginal tax rates of over 100 percent. That is, she pays in taxes and loses in benefits $1 or more for each additional dollar she might earn. Obviously, this is a severe disincentive to work and get off welfare.

The table on page 53 illustrates the problem, using, as an example, figures for the state of Pennsylvania. As one can see, a single mother with two children would receive $7,548 in benefits if she had zero earnings. If she goes out and earns $2,000, the combination of taxes and lower benefits raises her disposable income by just $1,375. This is equivalent to a tax rate of 31.25 percent on the earnings.

However, on the range of earnings between $5,000 and $8,000 per year, the marginal tax rate rises to well over 80 percent. In other words, out of each additional dollar she earns, her disposable income rises by less than 20 cents. Thus a woman earning $8,000 per year is just $2,408 better off than the woman earning nothing. This is equivalent to an effective tax rate of 70 percent.

Similar situations arise across the country, with only the degree varying from state to state.

De facto marginal tax rates are inherent in the nature of all means-tested welfare programs. The more quickly benefits are phased-out, the higher the implicit tax rate. Reducing benefits more gradually reduces the implicit tax rate, but necessarily raises the level of earnings one can have and still receive benefits.

The Congress is making a major effort to reform welfare to enable states to try alternative systems, and this is commendable. However, the best answer to this problem is strong economic growth and a sharp increase in higher-paying jobs. Other steps, such as deductibility of payroll taxes to ease that tax's burden on low-income workers, would be helpful as well.

EARNINGS AND DISPOSABLE INCOME FOR A SINGLE MOTHER WITH TWO CHILDREN IN PENNSYLVANIA

Earnings	Disposable Income	Marginal Rate	Effective Rate
0	$7,548	—	—
$2,000	$8,923	31.25	31.25
$4,000	$9,290	63.3	56.45
$5,000	$9,473	81.7	61.5
$6,000	$9,657	81.6	64.8
$7,000	$9,840	81.7	67.2
$8,000	$9,956	88.4	69.9
$9,000	$10,523	43.4	66.9
$10,000	$10,937	58.6	66.1
$15,000	$12,606	66.6	66.3

Source: Congressional Research Service, as published in the 1994 Green Book, p. 335.

For more information, contact:
Bruce Bartlett, National Center for Policy Analysis.
Phone: (703) 739-1527. Fax: (703) 739-5844.

WHY CAPITAL MATTERS

Capital is the engine of a growing economy. A recent study by Dale Jorgenson, chairman of the Department of Economics at Harvard University, showed that almost half of the growth of the American economy between 1948 and 1980 was directly attributable to the increase in U.S. capital formation (with most of the rest a result of increases and improvements in the labor force).[1]

It is common to think of capital as money, such as dollars invested in the stock market or in a business. To economists, capital refers to investments in physical capital, such as buildings and machines, as well as human capital—investments in time and tuition in acquiring valuable skills. Factories, office buildings, computers, tractors and trucks are all capital investments that increase the economy's ability to produce and distribute more and better goods and services to consumers at the lowest possible cost.

The ultimate source of capital improvement is the human mind. America's greatest economic asset is our people. Knowledge is capital. Invention is capital. Technological improvement is capital. The spirit of entrepreneurship is capital. The spark of an idea that leads to a new business or a new way of doing things is capital. Ten years ago when Bill Gates decided to form a computer softwear company and then invented MS-DOS, he was creating capital. So were the original investors who put money behind Microsoft. Thanks to the vision of Bill Gates and the risk-taking of his investors, Microsoft is now a globally dominant American firm employing 15,000 U.S. workers at high wages.

Between 1900 and 1990 real wages in the United States have risen about sixfold. In other words, a worker today earns as much in ten minutes as a worker in 1900 earned in an hour. What explains this surge in the living standards of the American worker? Primarily capital and productivity. U.S. workers are more productive, and their real wages are higher than those of workers in most other nations, because America has one of the highest ratios of capital per worker in the world.

Farming is a clear example. Today, the American farmer is by far the most productive in the world. Imagine what would happen to the productivity and output of American farmers today if they lacked modern irrigation systems, tractors, combines, and other sophisticated farm machinery. They would be no more productive than farmers in the poorest agrarian countries. Modern farm equipment and techniques are forms of capital.

Punitive taxes on capital are often advocated out of a misplaced belief that the returns from capital accrue primarily to the presumably wealthy owners of capital, such as stockholders or owners of businesses. To the extent that tax policy discourages capital accumulation, however, productivity and real wages will stagnate or decline. Nobel laureate Paul Samuelson explained the process as follows: "What happens to the wage rate when each person works with more capital goods? Because each worker has more capital to work with, his or her marginal product [or productivity] rises. Therefore, the competitive real wage rises as workers become worth more to capitalists and meet with spirited bidding up of their market wage rates."[2]

The graph on page 56 confirms that capital formation is the key ingredient to rising wages. Over the past fifty years, 90 percent of the variation in real wages is explained by the ratio of capital to labor. When there is more capital per worker, wages rise. Whenever the ratio of capital worker stops rising, wages stagnate. When capital taxes are running high and investment capital grows scarce, the last areas that will receive funds from the shrinking investment pool will be low-income, inner-city neighborhoods.

Human capital is also critical to increasing productivity and living standards. Sophisticated, high-tech equipment requires skilled workers, and skilled workers need the best equipment. Human capital includes education, training, and experience. If workers are more skilled, they will produce more and thus command higher salaries.

Under current law, those who save and invest in business capital are subjected to numerous overlapping taxes on corporate earnings, dividends, capital gains, and estates. Those who invest time and money in improving their own human capital are subjected to the highest marginal tax rates during their peak earning years. By discouraging improvements in physical and human capital, such tax policies slow the growth of the economy and of real wages.

CAPITAL-TO-LABOR RATIO AND REAL WAGE RATES

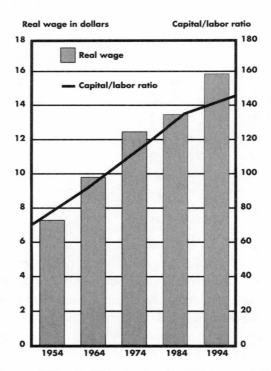

Source: Aldona and Gary Robbins, Institute for Policy Innovation, TaxAction Analysis. Private Sector Only.

Notes

1. Dale Jorgenson, *Productivity, Vol. 1: Postwar U.S. Economic Growth* (Cambridge, Massachusetts: MIT Press, 1995).

2. Paul Samuelson and William D. Nordhaus, *Economics* (New York: McGraw-Hill, 1985), p. 789.

For more information, contact:

Stephen Moore, The Cato Institute, 1000 Massachusetts Avenue, N.W., Washington, D.C. 20001. Phone: (202) 842-0200.

ESTIMATES VS. REALITY

Efforts to reform the tax system to promote efficiency and growth and to raise the incomes of all Americans have continually been thwarted by seriously deficient estimates of the revenue cost to the federal government. Revenue estimates tend to be "static" in the sense that they routinely ignore the effect of tax changes on the level of total economic activity—on the aggregate production, employment, and income of the population. Consequently, they overstate the revenue loss from tax rate reductions that can trigger substantial economic growth, and overstate the revenue gains from tax rate increases that can depress economic activity. Revenue estimators also tend to understate the degree to which people can avoid taxes by reducing the percent of their income taken in taxable form or altering the timing of their income.

Before taking such estimates too seriously, it is prudent to keep in mind the following warnings of Don Fullerton of the University of Virginia:

> First, each revenue estimate is only an estimate. It is an imperfect best guess made by an arbitrarily assigned estimator who uses old data, a set of arbitrary assumptions, and error-prone computer calculations. A different estimator could easily make other reasonable assumptions and get a different answer.
>
> Second, these revenue estimates are always relative to existing law, as if that were some valuable standard by which to judge all changes. There is nothing absolute about current law, for that is why changes are being considered in the first place.[1]

WHY WE NEED DYNAMIC, NOT STATIC REVENUE ESTIMATES: ACCOUNTING FOR GROWTH

A single, low marginal tax rate in a system that was not biased against saving and investment would substantially increase incentives to work, save, and invest. Professor Dale Jorgenson, chairman of the economics department at Harvard University, estimates that such a system could ultimately boost the annual output of the economy by about 15–20 percent on a permanent basis. Note that an increase of that magnitude would bring in substantial additional revenue to the federal government, enough to lower the tax rate by several percentage points. Failure to take these revenues into account would discourage tax reform and block the potential gains in income and employment. Just as static revenue estimates invariably exaggerate any revenue loss from lower tax rates, they likewise exaggerate the revenue gains from higher tax rates.[2] Relying on the estimates thus introduces a stubborn statistical bias in favor of higher tax rates.

So many potentially important revenue-increasing effects of a new tax system are completely ignored in the process of estimating tax receipts that it makes little sense to demand that a new tax system be "revenue neutral" in this static sense—as defined by government bookkeepers. The current tax system is suffocating the economy and encouraging tax avoidance and evasion. A tax system conducive to more rapid economic growth and reduced tax avoidance will generate far more revenue over time than the current law.

Past experience with static revenue estimates should generate some healthy skepticism. From 1981 to 1988, the highest tax rate fell from 70 percent to 28 percent, and rates were generally reduced across the board. Estimates prepared before the tax reduction suggested that revenue growth would be impaired. Yet, measured in constant 1987 dollars, federal revenues were $916.2 billion in 1989, up 27 percent from $719.2 billion in 1979, the peak of the previous economic expansion. In 1993, by contrast, real revenues were only $921.9 billion, barely changed from the 1989 level.[3]

Where tax rates were increased by the 1986 law, on the other hand, revenues came in far below the estimates. In 1987 dollars, revenue from the capital gains tax jumped from $28 billion in 1985 to $54.3 billion in 1986. By 1990–93, however, real capital gains tax receipts averaged only $24.6 billion per year.[4] Federal revenues from the individual income tax declined from 8.6 percent of GDP in 1989 to 8.2 percent in 1994, after two seemingly large increases in individual tax rates in 1990 and 1993.

It is still commonly believed that lowering the highest tax rates would lower revenues, with the result that middle incomes would supposedly bear a larger share of the burden. Yet the experience of the United States, Britain, and other nations is the exact opposite: Reducing unnecessarily high tax rates greatly *increases* the amount collected at higher incomes, and thereby allows more generous tax relief for those with middle or lower incomes.[5] Again, estimates prepared prior to the 1981 tax cuts, which reduced the highest tax rates from 70 percent to 28 percent, suggested that less revenue would be collected from those with higher incomes. By 1988, however, the top one percent of taxpayers were actually paying 27.5 percent of all individual income tax—up from 17.6 percent in 1981.

Revenue estimators object to having their methods described as "static." They point out, correctly, that they do take into account the fact that a higher excise tax will reduce sales of the taxed product, or that a higher capital gains tax will reduce the amount of gains that are realized each year—but always assuming an unchanged level of total employment and gross domestic product (GDP). But this was never what the critics meant by static revenue estimates. When economists outside the government refer to "dynamic" revenue effects, they mean that lower marginal tax rates and less hostile taxation of saving and investment will increase total GDP. They will increase GDP by increasing the percentage of adults who are willing to work, the intensity and skill of work, the amount of personal and business saving, the amount of investment (including investment in education), risk-taking by entrepreneurs and investors, and the efficiency with which labor and capital are used.

Congressional Budget Office economists William Randolph and Diane Lim Rogers recently surveyed some recent evidence on the impact of taxation, concluding that avoiding "accounting for saving and labor-supply behavior . . . cannot be justified based on existing studies."[6] So why are such effects nonetheless routinely ignored? The usual explanation is tradition and convention. "Traditional estimating conventions," explains a recent report from the Joint Committee on Taxation, "assume that tax law changes will have no overall effect on economic aggregates such as gross domestic product (GDP)."

"Following the standard revenue estimating conventions," says a memo from the Office of Tax Analysis, "the macroeconomic aggregates, such as the level of compensation, prices, employment, and gross domestic product, have been assumed to be unchanged by the proposal."[7]

Estimates have always been done this way. It is indeed standard, conventional and traditional. When it comes to estimating the impact of an entirely new system, however, such an appeal to orthodoxy is fatally flawed. Imagine using these estimating conventions to estimate the impact of replacing income taxes with a national sales tax. If prices were "assumed to be unchanged by the proposal," then how could businesses recoup the cost of a new sales tax? If they did so by cutting wages, how could compensation or employment be "assumed to be unchanged"? If prices are assumed to not rise and wages assumed to not fall, then this hypothetical sales tax must initially fall entirely on profits. In that case, how could investment and GDP be "assumed to be unchanged"? When it comes to estimating the impact of entirely new tax systems, the conventional conventions are not simply misleading but meaningless. They put aside all of the most important questions by assuming them out of existence.

Revenue estimators sometimes excuse the fact that economic consequences are ignored in the aggregate by the assertion that most benefits will take more than five years to fully take effect, which is beyond the usual budget planning period. Ignoring the long-run benefits from a less hostile policy toward working and saving is even more risky than pretending the effects do not exist. Myopic revenue estimates may thwart sound policies that are most likely to generate the most revenue in the long run, in favor of gimmicks that might *appear* to raise estimated revenue in the short run, while eventually losing revenue by damaging economic growth.

By increasing the incentive and ability to save, and to invest time and money in education and training, a tax system that taxes income only once, and does so at a single low rate, will greatly enlarge and improve the economy's stock of capital and human capital. That, in turn, will raise output per worker (productivity) and thus increase real wages. None of these effects are ever considered in revenue estimates or distribution tables. Tax burdens are distributed based on *existing* incomes, for example, even though making it easier to *increase* income and wealth is a major objective of a new tax system.

It may not yet be technically feasible to estimate the exact impact of tax policy on savings, employment, interest rates and production. It is, however, possible to estimate the *direction* and general magnitude of such effects through the use of models that appropriately account for the manner in which tax changes alter incentives to supply labor and capital. At a minimum, traditional, static estimates should carry explicit warning labels about what is left out of the calculations, and an informed judgment about the direction and likely magnitude of the resulting errors.[8]

A savings-neutral tax with a single low rate will result in a very significant, sustained increase in the amount of income that is both earned and reported.[9] If "traditional" (static) estimates conclude that this or that specific single tax rate would be "revenue neutral," experience teaches that such a rate would most likely result in a very substantial increase in real tax receipts over time.[10]

WHY WE NEED DYNAMIC, NOT STATIC REVENUE ESTIMATES: REPORTING MORE INCOME AND REDUCING TAX AVOIDANCE

The federal income tax on individuals has always hovered around 9–10 percent of personal income ever since the Korean War—regardless of whether the top tax rate was 92 percent or 28 percent, and regardless of whether so-called loopholes were opened or closed. From 1951 to 1994, receipts from the individual income tax have never been lower than 9 percent of personal income, and briefly reached 11 percent in only two recession years, 1969 and 1981.[11]

Since the federal tax on individual incomes has been almost constant as a percentage of personal income, the revenue yield from this tax mostly depends on (1) the proportion of personal income that is reported and taxed, and (2) the growth of personal income. High, graduated tax rates are damaging in both respects. High tax rates encourage people to minimize the proportion of income that is reported as taxable, and also to avoid doing any extra working or saving that would cause personal (and national) income to rise. In 1993, individual income taxes brought in only 9.2 percent of personal income, down from 10.1 percent in 1988. Growth of real GDP also slowed from 3.8 percent a year in 1983–89 to only 2.5 percent from the second quarter of 1991 to the third quarter of 1995.[12]

Revenue estimates rarely take much notice, if any, of the well documented fact that higher tax rates increase tax avoidance and evasion, and lower tax rates reduce the incentive to maximize deductions or to cheat. There are many ways in which people can minimize the proportion of income that is reported as taxable. These behavior changes need to be taken into account in the revenue estimates.

Taxable income in 1992 was only 46.5 percent of all personal income, down from 50.8 percent in 1988. The wider gap between personal income and taxable income partly reflects more intense use of deductions. High tax rates also increase the incentive to become more aggressive in seeking legal and illegal ways to minimize the tax bite. And high tax rates increase the attractiveness of tax-financed entitlements, compared with taxable work and saving. Government transfer payments (most of which are taxed lightly, if at all) rose from 14.3 percent of personal income in 1989 to 16.9 percent in 1994. With a single, low tax rate, people will have much less incentive to take their income in ways that escape taxes (including transfer payments and the underground economy), and much more incentive to earn more.

Revenue estimates rarely consider the fact that what happens to one tax is likely to alter behavior and affect revenues from another tax. Douglas Bernheim has shown that reduction of the tax rate on estates can be expected to increase revenues from the individual income tax, due to reduced incentives for aggressive estate planning.[13] Since tax proposals are usually examined one at a time, "general equilibrium" questions about the eventual impact on the entire tax base are neglected. This can be a serious problem when evaluating proposals to completely rebuild the tax system. Partly because of widespread tax arbitrage, Roger Gordon and Joel Slemrod estimated that "abandoning entirely any attempt to tax capital income . . . would have resulted in a slight rise in government revenue."[14] Gordon and Slemrod found that the *apparent* reduction in revenue from eliminating all capital taxes would be more than offset by increased revenue from other taxes. Traditional revenue estimates would not reveal such an effect, which creates a systematic bias against reducing or eliminating inefficient taxes.

Another source of estimating bias is the practical necessity of ignoring effects that are difficult to measure. It is well known that a capital-importing country like the U.S. can collect more revenue from a territorial tax system than under the current residence-based system.[15] However, there is no past experience to use in making a reliable estimate of exactly how much more revenue a territorial system may yield. Whenever there is no sound basis for making an estimate, such complex effects are usually ignored. When switching to an entirely new system, nearly every change is without precedent. That means what is ignored is likely to be more important than what is counted.

Even aside from the impact of a new tax system on capital formation and work incentives (which estimators *always* ignore), there are many potentially important ways in which various alternatives to the current tax regime might be expected to increase tax revenues. Because there is no precedent, however, these revenue-improving effects are inherently difficult to quantify. They include: (1) improving compliance by reducing complexities; (2) reducing the incentive and opportunity to maximize deductions and other avoidance devices; and (3) ending opportunities to avoid taxes by setting up different types of business entities, or by shifting income into low-tax years and deductible expenses into high-tax years. Because even such "microeconomic" issues are hard to quantify, they are unlikely to be considered in estimates of revenues.

Estimates of revenues and tax burdens employ flawed models *based on past experience* to predict or "simulate" what would happen under an entirely different tax structure and tax rate. When it comes to major changes in the tax structure and rates, very little can be estimated on the basis of past experience. Nobel Laureate Robert Lucas demonstrated that such statistical exercises are inherently flawed, because human behavior under one system will be quite different under another. "Simulations using these models can, in principle, provide no useful information as to the actual consequences of alternative economic policies," wrote Professor Lucas, "[These] kinds of policy simulations . . . are meaningless." [16]

Notes

1. Don Fullerton, "Inputs to Tax Policymaking: the Supply Side, the Deficit, and the Level of the Playing Field," NBER Working Paper No. 3507, November 1990, p. 59.

2. Martin Feldstein, "What the 1993 Tax Increases Really Did," *The Wall Street Journal,* October 25, 1995.

3. *Budget of the United States Government: Historical Tables,* 1996, table 1.3, p. 17.

4. Capital gains tax receipts from the Office of Tax Analysis, U.S. Treasury. Adjusted for inflation by the deflator used in the source cited in the previous note.

5. "In 1979–80, prior to the 1979 tax cut which lowered Britain's top marginal tax rate from 83 percent to 60 percent, the top 1 percent of taxpayers in Britain paid a 10.4 percent of total revenues collected. In 1985–86, six years after lowering the rates, the top 1 percent of taxpayers paid 12 percent of total revenues." Lawrence Lindsey, "The Laffer Curve: A Look at the Evidence," *London Conference on Taxes and Growth,* Manhattan Institute, 1986, p. 34. Hong Kong has a maximum tax of 15 percent on individuals, 16.5 percent on corporations, and no Social Security, estate, capital gains, or dividends tax. Revenues in Hong Kong quadrupled between 1983 and 1992, in U.S. dollars. Asian Development Bank, *Key Indicators,* 1993, p. 113.

6. William C. Randolph and Diane Lim Rogers, "The Implications for Tax Policy of Uncertainty About Labor Supply and Savings Responses," *National Tax Journal,* September 1995, p. 438.

7. Office of Tax Analysis, "Preliminary Analysis of a Flat Rate Consumption Tax," March 10, 1995.

8. A recent Congressional Budget Office report, for example, notes that "higher tax rates can reduce incentives to work and save, and encourage taxpayers to shift from taxable to nontaxable forms." CBO, *Reducing the Deficit: Spending and Revenue Options,* February 1995, p. 336.

9. The zero-sum notion that more savings and investment means less consumption is false. Savings provide the means by which real output and incomes increase. And rising incomes, in turn, permit more saving. From 1985 to 1993, gross investment increased by 2.5 percent a year in the U.S. and private consumption by 2.9 percent. In Singapore, investment grew by 5.7 percent a year and both private and government consumption grew by 6.3 percent. World Bank, *World Development Report: 1995,* table 8, p. 177.

10. Martin Feldstein, "The Effects of Marginal Tax Rates on Taxable Income: A Panel Study of the 1986 Tax Reform Act," NBER Working Paper No. 4496, October 1993.

11. *SOI Bulletin,* Winter 1994–95, table 8, p. 211.

12. Using the new chain-weighted GDP measure. *Economic Indicators,* November 1995, p.3.

13. B. Douglas Bernheim, "Does the Estate Tax Raise Revenue?" in Lawrence H. Summers, ed., *Tax Policy and the Economy,* NBER, vol. 1 (Cambridge, Massachusetts: MIT Press, 1987).

14. Roger H. Gordon and Joel Slemrod, "Do We Collect Any Revenue From Taxing Capital Income?" in Lawrence H. Summers, ed., *Tax Policy and the Economy*, NBER, p. 120. vol. 2 (Cambridge, Massachusetts: MIT Press, 1988).

15. "A territory-based tax system will provide larger revenues to capital importers than a residence based system." Jane G. Gravelle, *The Effects of Taxing Capital Income* (MIT Press, 1994), p. 234.

16. Robert E. Lucas, Jr., "Econometric Policy Evaluation: A Critique," in *Studies in Business Cycle Theory* (MIT Press, 1981), pp. 105, 111.

For more information, contact:

Alan Reynolds, The Hudson Institute, 1015 18th Street, N.W., Suite 200, Washington, D.C. 20036. Phone: (202) 223-7775.

TAX BIASES AGAINST SAVING AND INVESTMENT AND HOW TO FIX THEM

TAX BIASES ON INCOME THAT IS SAVED: FOUR LAYERS OF TAX

The income tax hits income that is saved and invested much harder than income used for consumption. The income tax is imposed on income that is saved and again on the income produced by the saving. In contrast, the income tax falls on income used for consumption but does not fall again on the consumption spending and the services and enjoyment it provides.

For example, if one uses after-tax income to buy a bond, the stream of interest payments is also taxed. If one uses after-tax income to buy a television, there is no additional tax on the purchase of the TV or the stream of entertainment it provides.

In fact, people who save and invest find their income subject to four layers of federal tax (versus one layer for consumption).

Layer 1—tax on earnings. The income is taxed when first earned.

Layer 2—tax on interest and business income. When the after-tax income is saved, the returns on the saving are taxed—double taxation. If the saver puts his or her income into a bond or bank account, the interest earned is taxed. If the saver invests directly in a small business, his or her investment income from the proprietorship or partnership is taxed. If the saver buys a share of corporate stock, he or she is in fact buying a share of the company, a claim to a share of its income, and his or her share of the corporate income tax on the corporate earnings.

Layer 3—taxes on dividends and capital gains. Shareholders face triple taxation. In addition to the original tax on the saving and the tax paid by the corporation, shareholders must pay personal income tax on any dividends that the corporation distributes out of its after-tax income. (This is sometimes called "the double taxation of dividends," but it is really the third layer of tax because the income used to buy the shares was taxed before it was saved.)

There is a third layer of income tax even if the corporation does not pay a dividend. If a corporation (or other business) retains its after-tax earnings for reinvestment, the earning power and the value of the business will increase. If the owner or shareholder sells the business or the shares, the increase in value is taxed as a capital gain.

Capital gains can arise whenever a business's prospects improve, not just because of reinvestment of previously taxed earnings. The development of a successful new product, or a discovery such as a new wonder drug or a new oil field, can boost the after-tax earnings outlook of a business and increase its current market value. If the higher expected business earnings come to pass, they will be taxed as corporate income and/or unincorporated business or personal income. To tax as well the increase in the business's current value if the business or the shares are sold is to double-tax the future income of the business before it even occurs, and to triple-tax the initial saving.[1] The current law income tax treatment of capital gains, whatever their source, is multiple taxation of saving.[2]

Layer 4—estate and gift taxes. If the saving outlives the saver, and the remaining unspent assets exceed a modest exempt amount, the federal unified transfer (estate and gift) tax imposes another layer of federal tax on the already multiply taxed saving.

ENDING THE TAX BIASES AGAINST SAVING AND INVESTMENT

These tax biases are real and they have serious consequences. Savers and investors expect a reasonable after-tax return on their assets. Because of these biases, saving and investment must earn substantially higher returns to cover the added taxes and still be worthwhile substitutes for consumption. Saving and investment earn higher returns only if the quantity of capital is significantly reduced, making the value of each additional unit's output that much greater. The current biases in the tax treatment of capital have cost the economy several trillion dollars in saving and investment, considerably retarding the growth of productivity, wages, and employment, and retarding the growth of individual income and wealth. It is no exaggeration to suggest that the level of income in the United States could be at least 15 percent to 20 percent higher than it is today if these biases did not exist. That missing income has simply been thrown away to no good purpose. These losses could amount to as much as $4,000–$6,000 per year for typical middle income families. The current system also cripples people's ability and incentive to save for retirement, leaving people with less retirement income than they need to be financially secure, and increasing their dependence on government programs or their children in old age.

Making the tax system even-handed or neutral between saving and investment on the one hand and consumption on the other requires several steps.

The transfer tax on estates and gifts must be eliminated. Most of an estate is saving that has already been taxed. There is no justice in taxing it again. Those elements of an estate that consisted of tax deferred saving should remain tax deferred so long as the heirs continue to save it. The current harsh treatment of estates makes elderly people fearful of holding on to their assets. Forcing them to divest their assets does them no service. The modest exempt amount in current law, $600,000, is a sum of money that would be wiped out in a decade if an elderly couple required nursing home care.

The dual taxation of corporate income at the corporate and individual level must be eliminated through "integration" of the individual and corporate income taxes (or the substitution of a non-income type of tax system). Integration means that corporate income is recognized as belonging to the shareholders, and is taxed either on individual tax returns or corporate tax returns, but not both.

The tax system must either allow savers to deduct saving or to exclude the returns on saving from taxable income. There must be no separate, additional taxation of capital gains. Investment outlays must be deducted in the year the outlay is made (expensed) rather than depreciated over time. Deducting saving and taxing the returns, as is done to a limited degree with pensions and IRAs, is one way to eliminate the basic tax bias against saving. Another method is to treat saving as we now treat tax exempt bonds; there is no deduction of the amount saved, but no taxation of the interest or other returns. The following section presents some simple examples to illustrate how a tax bias arises if these rules are broken, and why these treatments are the correct ones.

NEUTRAL TREATMENT OF INCOME
USED FOR SAVING AND CONSUMPTION

The income tax, by taxing both income that is saved and the returns on that income, taxes saving and investment more heavily than consumption. There are two ways to restore neutrality. One approach is to exclude saving from taxable income while taxing all returns on the saving. The other is to include saving in taxable income but impose no tax on the returns.

Deduct saving, tax returns method. Excluding (or deducting) saving and investment from taxable income is called "expensing." In the case of saving, expensing is akin to the tax-deferred treatment allowed limited amounts of retirement saving today (as with current IRAs, 401(k) plans, 403(b) plans, SEPs, and Keogh plans), but with no restrictions on the amount of saving that could be deducted, no penalty tax on withdrawal at any age, and no forced distribution at any age. In effect, the purchase of a bond, bank account, or share of stock would be recognized as a cost of earning income. When the outlay is made, it would be deducted. The returns (including interest, dividends, the return of the principal when the bond matures, or the proceeds from the sale of the stock at a later date) would be taxed, unless reinvested.

Tax saving, exempt returns method. The other route to neutrality is to tax the income that is to be saved, but exempt interest, dividends,

INCOME TAX BIAS AGAINST SAVINGS AND TWO CURES

Pre-tax income needed to have $100 for consumption after taxes or a $100 bond paying $4 in interest after taxes under ordinary income tax treatment, IRA-type treatment, or tax-exempt bond treatment

		PRE-TAX INCOME	TAX	AFTER-TAX INCOME	INTEREST ON SAVING	TAX ON INTEREST	AFTER-TAX INTEREST	INCREASE IN COST OF ACTIVITY DUE TO TAX
No income tax exists	Income consumed	$100	$0	$100	$4	—	—	—
	Income saved	$100	$0	$100	—	$0	$4	—
Ordinary income tax levied at 20% rate	Income consumed	$125	$25	$100	—	—	—	25%
	Income saved	$156.25	$31.25	$125	$5	$1	$4	56.25%
IRA-type treatment: amounts saved tax deductible, returns on saving taxed		$125	$0	$125	$5	$1	$4	25%
Tax-exempt bond treatment: no deduction of saving, returns not taxed		$125	$25	$100	$4	$0	$4	25%

The 20 percent income tax, by taxing income when first earned and taxing the return on saving, raises the cost of consumption by 25 percent and the cost of obtaining additional future income by 56.25 percent, more than twice the increase in the cost of consumption. Under IRA or tax-exempt bond treatment, the tax raises the cost of obtaining additional future income by 25 percent, the same penalty as on consumption.

capital gains, and other returns on the saving from tax. This is akin to the tax treatment accorded state and local tax-exempt bonds. No deduction for buying the asset is allowed, but the returns are not taxed.

Both methods of dealing with saving eliminate the excess tax on income that is saved compared to income that is used for consumption. A tax increases the cost of any item or activity it is imposed upon. The income tax is biased because it raises the cost of saving and investment more than it raises the cost of consumption. Let's look at how much more a person must earn to support a given level of consumption after a tax is imposed, compared to how much more he or she must earn to buy an asset that delivers a given amount of after-tax income. (See table on page 71.)

Suppose that, if there were no income tax, one could buy $100 of consumption goods or a $100 bond paying 4 percent interest, or $4 a year. Now impose a 20 percent income tax. One would have to earn $125, and give up $25 in tax, to have $100 of after-tax income to consume. The pre-tax cost of $100 of consumption has risen 25 percent. To get a $4 interest stream, after taxes, one would have to earn $5 in interest, pre-tax. But $5 in interest requires a $125 bond. To buy a $125 bond, one would have to earn $156.25 and pay $31.25 in tax. The cost of the after-tax interest stream has gone up 56.25 percent, more than twice the increase in the cost of consumption. Put another way, if there were no income tax, obtaining a $1 stream of interest would cost the saver $25 in current consumption ($100/$4). After the income tax, it would take $156.25 to buy a $4 interest stream or $125 of consumption. Each $1 interest stream would cost $31.25 in foregone consumption ($125/$4), 25 percent more than in the no-tax situation.

There are two ways to restore neutrality. One is to exempt interest from tax, as with state and local tax-exempt bonds. One would then have to earn $125 to buy a $100 bond, earning $4 with no further tax. The other method is to allow a deduction for income that is saved, while taxing the returns, as with a deductible IRA. One would have to earn $125 to buy a $125 bond, earning $5 in interest pre-tax, and, after paying $1 in tax on the interest, have $4 left.[3]

NEUTRAL TREATMENT OF INVESTMENT: EXPENSING

Expensing is the simplest and most sensible way to provide unbiased tax treatment of direct investment in physical capital. Just as neutral treatment of saving can be accomplished by deducting saving and taxing the returns, neutral treatment of investment can be achieved by expensing investment and taxing the returns. Expensing means writing off the investment in the year it is purchased rather than the current practice of stretching out capital consumption (depreciation) allowances over an extended period of time, which reduces their value. The stretch-out constitutes an interest-free loan to the Treasury of the taxes that would otherwise have been saved by the deduction. Outlays for plant, equipment, buildings and other structures, land, inventory, and research and development should all be deductible in the year the outlays are made, just as for any other production input. Subsequently, all the returns on these investments, including sales of goods and services, rents, and royalties (all net of other costs), and sales of assets, should be taxed.

Under current law, purchases of equipment are written off over periods of time ranging from three to twenty years. Most structures are written off over a thirty-nine-year period. Stretching out the write-off period reduces the present value of the deductions due to lost interest and inflation. The result is that the business deducts an amount that is less in present value than the value of the equipment. The under-depreciation overstates taxable income, resulting in a higher-than-statutory tax rate on the real earnings of the asset. The table on page 74 illustrates the difference in the value of the deductions between expensing and one of the set of depreciation schedules commonly used in current law. For example, the present value of deductions for the seven-year asset at 3 percent inflation and a 3.5 percent real discount rate is only 84.6 percent of the cost of the asset. The present value falls short of expensing by $15.40 on a $100 piece of equipment, costing the firm an extra $5.39 in tax in present value terms, assuming a 35 percent corporate tax rate. The longer the life of the asset, the greater is the loss of value of the write-off.[4]

PRESENT VALUE OF CURRENT LAW CAPITAL CONSUMPTION ALLOWANCES PER DOLLAR OF INVESTMENT COMPARED TO EXPENSING (FIRST-YEAR WRITE-OFF)

Asset lives:		3 years	5 years	7 years	10 years	15 years	20 year
Present value of first-year write-off of $1 of investment:		$1.00	$1.00	$1.00	$1.00	$1.00	$1.00
Present value of current law write-off of $1 if inflation rate is:	0%	$0.964	$0.937	$0.912	$0.877	$0.796	0.742
	3%	$0.935	$0.888	$0.846	$0.789	$0.667	$0.592
	5%	$0.917	$0.859	$0.807	$0.739	$0.599	$0.519

Assumes a 3.5 percent real discount rate, assets purchased in first quarter of the year.

Depreciation schedules under the alternative minimum tax (AMT) are even less favorable than those allowed under the regular income tax. The AMT is designed to make businesses and individuals pay some tax each year even if legitimate business deductions reduce their ordinary taxable income to zero. It must be understood that, in reality, revenues are not income until they exceed the cost of producing the income. By holding deductible costs below actual costs, ordinary depreciation and AMT depreciation schedules overstate businesses' and individuals' real incomes. When income is overstated for tax purposes, the tax is a bigger percent of the taxpayer's true income than the statutory tax rate. The overstatement of income sometimes turns a real loss into an apparent profit and forces a tax payment when none should be due.

A tax system that does not allow full and immediate write-offs for capital costs is biased against investment relative to consumption and against investment in long-lived assets relative to short-lived assets. The current tax treatment of depreciation diverts economic activity in the

United States away from capital-intensive industries such as manufacturing, especially heavy industry, and into services and less capital-intensive production. In the process, many high-value added jobs have been lost.

Accountants and tax officials often argue for delaying write-offs to correspond with the gradual decline in an asset's future earning power as the asset wears out. This so-called "economic depreciation" is fine for measuring the size of the country's capital stock and the level of economic capacity, but it has nothing to do with appropriately measuring the taxable income of an individual or business, which is revenues less costs. When a business (or its lenders and shareholders) buys a machine or other asset, it gives up the resources to pay for it at the moment the payment is made, not several years later. It must immediately forego all other possible uses of the money, including earning interest, hiring labor, buying inventory, or distributing dividends to shareholders to save or consume as they see fit. Furthermore, the seller of the machine must take the sales revenue into taxable income immediately. The asymmetrical treatment by the Treasury of the buyer and the seller—partial write-off for the buyer, full taxation of the purchase price for the seller—is clearly arbitrary, inappropriate, and anti-investment. Only expensing measures income correctly and imposes the correct amount of tax.

Notes

1. A capital gain on a bond, stock, or sale of an unincorporated business or other property is not an additional amount of income above and beyond the interest or business income underlying the assets. The current price of an asset is the value that people put on the future income the asset will generate after taxes. Asset prices change if the expected future after-tax earnings change. If a stock's future annual earnings are expected to be $5 a share before taxes, and (assuming a 20 percent tax rate) $4 a share after taxes, and if the "discount rate" (the rate of return that people demand to receive to compensate them for the use of their resources and inflation) is 10 percent, then the share price will be $40 (because $40 at 10 percent yields $4 a year). The $40 stock price is the "present value" of an indefinite stream of $4 in after-tax future earnings. If the business announces a new product and its projected income doubles to $10 a share before tax and $8 after-tax, the

share price will about double to $80. If the earnings projections come true, the additional $5 in annual income will be taxed, yielding the Treasury an additional $1 a year. The additional $4 in after-tax future earnings are worth $40 at the present time. If that $40 jump in the share price is taxed as a capital gain (an $8 tax at a 20 percent rate), it constitutes an extra layer of tax on the additional after-tax future income, equivalent to raising the tax rate on the $5 pre-tax income stream from 20 percent to 36 percent. (The $8 capital gains tax is equivalent to $.80 a year, on top of the $1 income tax on the earnings. $1.80/$5 = 36 percent.)

2. Additional equally unjustified extra layers of tax can sneak in when corporations hold stock in other companies. If Company A holds less than 80 percent of the stock of Company B, then Company A must pay tax on 30 percent of dividends it receives from Company B before passing the dividends on to its own shareholders for additional taxation. Any capital gains tax paid by a corporation is also an unjustified additional layer of tax on saving.

3. For a fuller discussion of the basic income tax bias against saving and investment, see: David F. Bradford, et al *Blueprints for Basic Tax Reform,* second edition, revised (Arlington, Virginia, Tax Analysts, 1984); Michael A. Schuyler, *Consumption Taxes: Promises & Problems* (Washington, D.C.: Institute for Research on the Economics of Taxation, 1984); *Tax Reform for Fairness, Simplicity, and Growth, Vol. 3, Value-Added Tax* (Washington, D.C.: Department of the Treasury, 1984); Norman B. Ture and Stephen J. Entin, *Save, America* (Washington, D.C.: Institute for Research on the Economics of Taxation, 1989); Norman B. Ture and B. Kenneth Sanden, *The Effects of Tax Policy on Capital Formation* (New York: Financial Executives Research Foundation, 1977).

4. In theory, the present value of deferred write-offs could be made equal to expensing by paying appropriate interest on the write-offs, as in the various "neutral cost recovery systems" that have been proposed in recent years. Alternatively, a schedule of investment tax credits could be designed, one for each asset life, to offset the bias. The former approach is complicated and the interest rate might not match the discount rate (adjusted for risk and opportunity cost) of the investor. The latter approach would require adjusting the ITC every time the inflation rate changed. Expensing is simple, unbiased, and foolproof.

For more information, contact:
Stephen J. Entin, Institute for Research on the Economics of Taxation, 1300 19th Street, N.W., Suite 240, Washington, D.C. 20036. Phone: (202) 463-1400.

GROWTH-FRIENDLY TAX SYSTEMS

There are several types of tax systems that successfully exclude saving and investment or their returns from tax, eliminate the bias against saving and investment, and simplify the tax system. These include two types of unbiased income taxes and various types of sales taxes. Each has advantages and disadvantages, but they all have one very important point in common: they are all unbiased taxes on labor and capital income, properly measured, either when earned or when spent. Whatever direction the tax restructuring movement takes, it is important to remember that all these approaches have this great common advantage over current law. All of the serious tax reform proposals that are being widely discussed around the country and in Washington employ one or more of these approaches in some form.

Saving-Deferred Income Tax.

Under the saving-deferred income tax, all labor and capital income would be taxed once and only once on individual tax returns. There would be personal exemptions and a tax rate structure that could be flat or graduated. (The commission favors a single rate.)[1] The distinctive feature of this system is that individuals would exclude their saving from taxable income; they would include the returns on their saving—interest, dividends, and sales of assets—in taxable income, but only if the returns were withdrawn for consumption, and not reinvested. Businesses would deduct their dividend payments as well as their interest payments, passing them on to shareholders and lenders for tax purposes. Any remaining capital earnings retained by the business for reinvestment would be tax-deferred on behalf of the shareholders, and investment would be expensed. Since all taxable capital income would be reported on individual tax returns, businesses would not need to file. Further details are presented below.

Returns-Exempt Income Tax.

The best known example of a returns-exempt income tax is the single-rate tax proposed by professors Robert Hall and Alvin Rabushka.[2] In its pure form it would have only one tax rate applicable to income over a large exempt amount, with no other deductions permitted. Only labor and pension income would be taxed on individual tax returns. In general, individuals would not deduct their saving, but would not be taxed on the earnings of the saving. (In legislative variations of this proposal, contributions to pensions and other retirement plans would remain deductible, and the withdrawals taxable, as under current law.) All income from capital would be taxed once and only once on business tax returns. Business would expense investment outlays and other costs, and pay tax on all the returns. Some possible variations of the tax, allowing some deductions, are presented below.

Sales Tax.

Taxes imposed on the sales of goods and services, such as a retail sales tax or a manufacturers excise tax, allow individuals to defer tax on their saving until the saving is withdrawn for consumption. A national retail sales tax, if it were to exclude investment goods from the sales tax base, would be neutral between income used for saving and investment and income used for consumption.[3]

THE NATURE OF THE TAXES

One point of clarification is in order. Various types of sales taxes and excise taxes are often referred to as "consumption taxes," rather than income taxes, because they are collected when products are produced or sold. A broadly imposed national retail sales tax would fall on an amount of GNP that equals total consumption. Nonetheless, these are not taxes on the act of consumption or on the goods and services consumed. Goods and services do not pay taxes. Only people pay taxes. All taxes, in fact, are taxes on income. Sales and excise taxes either depress sales of the taxed products, reducing the incomes of the people who provide the labor and capital used to make them, or they reduce the purchasing power of that income when the workers and savers attempt to spend it.

The two neutral income-style taxes are imposed on income as it is earned, with the amount saved and invested excluded (or the earnings of saving excluded). Saving and investment are outlays that people make to earn income. There is no real income or profit from saving and investment until the returns exceed the outlays. Consequently, taxing that part of the payments to labor and capital left over after saving and investment is the correct amount of income from labor and capital to tax. (Alternatively, the saving should be taxed, and the returns exempted.) These systems are sometimes called "consumption-based income taxes" or "saving-deferred income taxes." Excluding from total income the amount that is saved and used to finance investment leaves an amount equal in a given time period to total consumption. This does not convert the tax into a consumption tax, however; it is merely a means of avoiding multiple taxation of income used for saving, and the returns on the saving will be taxed when earned, unless reinvested in turn. It bears repeating that all taxes are paid out of income by people, not by businesses, and not by goods and services.

BENEFITS IN COMMON—ENDING TAX BIASES AND PROMOTING SIMPLICITY

Each of these tax systems eliminates the tax bias against saving and investment found in the current income tax. Each can readily accommodate a single low tax rate on all taxpayers. Each can substantially reduce the confusing treatment of foreign source income that cripples American firms attempting to compete abroad. Each system would eliminate the alternative minimum tax and the estate tax. The systems would have expensing instead of depreciation (or equivalent non-taxation of investment outlays), and no separate taxation of capital gains. Many of the major sources of complexity in the current tax code would be gone.

SOME DIFFERENCES TO CONSIDER

While sharing many advantages, some of these tax systems do better than others when measured against the other important tax policy considerations. Among these are simplicity, visibility, and fairness. The integrated saving-deferred income tax and, to a large extent, the returns-exempt income tax show the cost of government pretty clearly, and can easily exempt low-income citizens. Sales taxes tend to be hidden in the cost of goods and services, making the cost of government less visible.[4] They are the easiest taxes for individuals to comply with—individuals are totally divorced from the collection process—but they may go too far in that regard. Sales taxes also pose some problems with respect to easing their burden on low-income taxpayers and compliance costs of businesses. Some additional work on these issues is needed. Sales taxes may be imposed on imports and remitted or not levied on exports. This feature is called border adjustability, or being "destination-based." These taxes may also be set up without border adjustability, in which case they are called "origin-based." The question of border adjustment should not be the determining consideration in choosing which tax system to adopt.[5]

A CLOSER LOOK AT THE SAVING-DEFERRED TAX AND RETURNS-EXEMPT TAX

Both types of unbiased income tax can be constructed with an exempt amount for people with low income and a single rate for incomes above the exempt amount. The single rate would eliminate the graduated tax rate bias against work, education, risk taking, and success. Neither would discriminate or double tax income used for saving and investment. Both would be significantly simpler, over all, than current law.

In both systems, all income would be taxed, but only once. The income from investment—which belongs to the savers (lenders, shareholders, and owners of noncorporate business) who financed the investment—would be taxed either on the savers' tax returns after it is distributed by the businesses, or on the businesses' tax returns before it is distributed to the savers, but not both. Whichever approach is taken, it would be incorrect to conclude that capital income was escaping tax because it did not appear on one tax form or the other. The only reason that income from capital appears on both types of tax form under current law is that current law double- and triple-taxes income that is saved.

Saving-Deferred Tax.

The theory behind the saving-deferred tax (also known as a cash flow tax or inflow-outflow tax) is that all income should be taxed as close to the final recipient of the income as possible, for maximum visibility. In its pure form, all inflows (all receipts) would be taxable, and all outflows (all outlays associated with earning the income, or any income given away to others, either voluntarily or as a tax) would be deductible.

Individuals would pay tax on labor income (wages, salaries, and the value of fringe benefits), the taxable portion of social security, and capital income (interest, dividends, pension income). Individuals would deduct their net saving (including purchases of stocks and bonds) or pay tax on their net withdrawals (including sales of assets).[6] There would be no separate calculation of capital gains; they would be covered in the proceeds from the sale of assets. Employers and financial institutions would report all these net amounts to the taxpayers on forms like those currently in use. Since all saving could be deducted in this system, all current-law restrictions on the amounts allowed as contributions and withdrawals under employer-sponsored pension plans should be eliminated.

Individuals would deduct personal allowances. In the pure form of this tax, deductions would include mortgage and other interest paid, charitable contributions, and, if allowed, the individual portion of payroll taxes and state and local taxes.[7] These deductions would be over and above the personal allowances.

There would be no separate taxation of businesses in a saving-deferred tax. Interest and dividends would be deductible by businesses in this tax system, passed on to lenders and shareholders to be taxed. The remaining earnings retained by the business for reinvestment would be treated as tax-deferred saving by the shareholders or other owners. These deductions would exhaust the earnings.[8]

In this system, the deduction for business investment would effectively be passed along to the savers who lend money to, buy shares in, or otherwise invest in the business. Savers would deduct their purchases of stocks and bonds. These proceeds of stock and bond issues, plus retained earnings, would be treated as taxable inflows to a business, but these sources of financing must just equal the (deductible) capital investment and net saving of the business, eliminating taxable business income. Consequently, there would be no need for businesses to file an income tax return, eliminating most of the accounting, auditing, and costs of enforcement and compliance in the current tax system.

In a sense, businesses would be treated like pensions or IRAs owned by the savers: all income individuals transfer to businesses through lending or the purchase of shares would be deductible by the savers; only those business earnings distributed to lenders and shareholders (and not reinvested) would be taxable, and would be reported on the individual tax returns.

Returns-Exempt or Modified Hall-Rabushka Tax.

The returns-exempt income tax would impose a single tax rate above a generous exempt amount. This system achieves simplification and unbiased treatment of saving by taxing only labor and pension income on individual tax returns and taxing all other income from capital on business returns. There would be no need for businesses, individuals, or the I.R.S. to track the payments of capital income from businesses to taxpayers. This method of achieving simplicity reduces the visibility of the tax on capital.

In one relatively pure form of the returns-exempt income tax, individuals who work would pay tax on wages, salaries, and the value of non-pension fringe benefits. Retirees would pay tax only on pension income (the only saving-related income taxed on individual returns). Social security benefits would not be taxable. There would generally be no deduction for non-pension saving, and no tax on the returns on the individual tax form. For simplicity, and to keep the tax rate low, the only deductions for individuals would be for a generous personal allowance and, possibly, liberalized pension plan contributions.[9] Since all saving is to receive neutral treatment in this system, it would make sense to eliminate all current-law restrictions on the amounts allowed as contributions and withdrawals under employer-sponsored pension plans.

In that same form of the tax, businesses would pay taxes on returns to capital before they are distributed to lenders, shareholders, or other owners (except for pension distributions taxed on individual returns). Businesses would not deduct interest or dividend payments, and would not pay tax on interest and dividends received. Deductions for fringe benefits and state and local taxes would be eliminated. Payroll taxes would not be deductible. However, businesses could expense all outlays on research and development and investment in plant, equipment, structures, inventory, and land. Net operating losses would be carried forward with interest.

Loss of the interest deduction for mortgages and businesses would be offset by elimination of the tax on interest received by lenders. Interest rates would be expected to fall to current after-tax levels, compensating borrowers for the loss of the deduction, and leaving lenders with the same after-tax return as under current law.

It is difficult to deal with banks, S&Ls, brokerage houses, and other financial intermediaries in any tax system in which interest is not generally deductible by borrowers and taxable to lenders, including the returns-exempt tax, sales taxes, or value-added taxes. A separate tax, based on inflow-outflow, would have to be used for these businesses.[10]

Variations on this system are possible. In its pure form, the Hall-Rabushka tax would have no itemized deductions for individuals. One variation would allow the retention of the charitable deduction and retention of the home mortgage interest deduction for borrowers.[11] (Retention of the mortgage interest deduction for borrowers has a limited revenue effect if the lenders are taxed on the interest as under current law.) Congress should consider how best to treat state and local income and property taxes. (See note 7, and background paper, below, for a more complete discussion of various itemized deductions for individuals and businesses under both tax systems.)

In its pure form, Hall-Rabushka would collect a greater amount of tax from business than current law. To avoid the need for changes in labor compensation agreements, retention of the payroll tax deduction for businesses could be considered. To diminish the adverse effect of the payroll tax on employment, the deduction could be extended to individuals as well, in exchange for continued but less onerous taxation of social security benefits. (The extension is feasible under either income tax system. See background paper, below, on the income tax treatment of payroll taxes and social security benefits.)

COMPARISON OF SAVING-DEFERRED TAX AND RETURNS-EXEMPT TAX

Advantages and Disadvantages of the Saving-Deferred Tax.

Of the two systems, the saving-deferred or inflow-outflow tax would make taxes somewhat more visible to taxpayers, because interest, dividends, and other returns on capital would be displayed on individual income tax forms. It would be somewhat more complex for individuals, but far less complex for businesses, than the other approach. Businesses would pass through all taxable income to individuals. Only distributions by businesses would be taxable; businesses would have far fewer accounting and compliance costs, and would not have to file federal tax returns. The deduction for investment in plant and equipment would be effectively shifted from businesses to the savers who provide the financing. This would be an advantage for start-up businesses that have little income as yet from previous investments against which to take a deduction. The inflow-outflow tax could handle financial businesses as easily as nonfinancial businesses.

Advantages and Disadvantages of the Returns-Exempt Tax.

The returns-exempt single rate tax would be simpler for individuals, but more complex for business, than the other approach. There would be fewer deductions to account for than under current law, and individuals would not have to report capital income—a simplification. Businesses would still have to file tax returns in this system; capital income would be reported on business tax returns, and the tax would be less visible to the ultimate owners. To make the tax on capital income visible to savers, businesses could be required to report the income and the tax to lenders and shareholders, for information only; the lenders and shareholders would not have to include it on their tax returns. The financial sector of the economy would have to be given the alternative inflow-outflow type of tax treatment.

KEY POINTS IN COMMON FOR THE SAVING-DEFERRED AND RETURNS-EXEMPT TAXES

Equivalence and Importance of the Approaches' Treatment of Saving.

The two methods are equivalent in their treatment of saving (if savers face the same tax rate over time), and better than current law. For example, suppose that interest rates are 7 percent. At that rate of interest, $1 saved would grow, with interest, to $2 in ten years. (Alternatively, suppose that reinvested earnings caused the price of a share of stock to double in ten years, and that the stock is sold and the capital gain is realized at that time.) Suppose also that the income tax rate is 20 percent

Under the saving-deductible method, an individual could earn $100, save it without paying tax up front on the deposit or on the annual interest build-up (or on the stock purchase and accruing gain), and withdraw $200 ten years later. After paying a 20 percent tax on the withdrawal (or the proceeds of the stock sale), the saver would have $160 to spend.

Under the exempt-returns method, an individual could earn $100, pay a 20 percent tax, and save the remaining $80. Without owing any further tax on the returns, he could withdraw $160 ten years later, and, here too, would have $160 to spend.

Either neutral method is better than current law. Under the current tax system, an individual earning $100 would have to pay a 20 percent tax, save $80, and owe tax annually on the interest, reducing the 7 percent interest rate to an after-tax rate of 5.6 percent. With less interest left to build up after taxes, the saver would accumulate only $138 to withdraw and spend after ten years. The $22 difference ($160-$138)

ADVANTAGE OF TAX-DEFERRED SAVING OVER CURRENT LAW'S DOUBLE TAXATION

BUILD-UP OF $1,000 SAVED PER YEAR

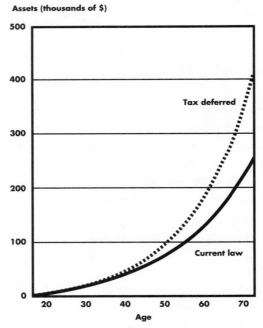

Saving from age 20 onward, under tax-deferred system and current law double taxation (hypothetical 20 percent tax rate).

between current law and the neutral systems (about 14 percent over 10 years) is a measure of the double taxation imposed by current law on income that is saved.

The penalty on saving under current law sharply retards the buildup of retirement saving that is not protected from double taxation by a pension plan. (See graph, on page 86.) A dollar saved at 7 percent interest, tax-deferred, at age 25 would compound to $16 at age 65, and to $32 at age 75, before tax. After a 20 percent tax on withdrawals, the saver would have $12.80 or $25.60 to spend. In an ordinary double-taxed bank account at 7 percent however, the spendable amount at age 65 would be only $8.83, or only $15.23 at age 70, about 30 percent and 40 percent less, respectively.

The enhanced ability to save for education, home ownership, and retirement would be an important feature of a restructured tax code. Retirement saving is a subject of great importance as the baby boom approaches old age. The Social Security System faces enormous deficits. Eliminating those deficits by means of large increases in the payroll tax would cost several million jobs. The Bipartisan Commission on Entitlement and Tax Reform has discussed increased reliance on private retirement saving as an alternative solution.[12]

Treatment of Capital Gains.

As the example above shows, the two methods produce the same after-tax returns on saving involving capital gains. In fact, under either the saving-deferred or returns-exempt approach to ending the tax bias, capital gains would cease to be a tax issue, greatly simplifying tax forms for individual and business taxpayers and reducing disputes with the I.R.S. Under the return-exempt approach, there would obviously be no tax on capital gains, because no returns on saving would be taxable. In the deductible-saving case, the purchase of the assets would be expensed (resulting in no basis for tax purposes), and all the proceeds of asset sales would be properly included in taxable income. Any gain or loss embedded in the numbers would be automatically calculated correctly for tax purposes, without any special calculations required. If the proceeds of asset sales were reinvested, any embedded gains could be rolled over, and would remain tax-deferred until withdrawn for consumption.

Growth and Job Creation.

Either of these income tax systems, or the national sales tax, would be far more conducive to growth than current law. They would allow the economy to gain, over about a decade, the investment and growth that the current biased tax system has suppressed. They take different approaches to eliminating the biases in current law. They have different transition problems, but none of these are unsolvable. The sooner that one of these approaches is adopted, the sooner the gains can be realized.

The potential for faster growth of jobs and incomes should allay concerns that tax reform might force a choice between higher short-term budget deficits and tax increases for some taxpayers. In particular, when we look at how tax reform affects a family or individual worker or taxpayer, it is not enough to apply the new tax code to last year's income because neither the economy nor the taxpayer will behave the same way after tax reform as before. As saving and investment increase, productivity and the taxpayer's income will grow faster for a decade or more and be higher by increasing amounts over time. The taxpayer will enjoy lower interest rates on mortgages and student loans as the tax burden on saving is reduced. Although reduced taxes on saving may not instantly lower the tax of a twenty-year-old who has not yet begun to save, it will lower taxes on that worker as he or she accumulates assets over a working lifetime, and leave that worker many tens of thousands, or even hundreds of thousands, of dollars better off by age 65, and far more secure in retirement (see graph on page 86). Whatever happens in the first year, people will enjoy a lifetime of benefits from a pro-growth tax reform, and it is the lifetime benefit that should be looked at.

As for the federal budget, there are many benefits, both short-term and long-term. People would immediately have less incentive to shelter their existing income from tax. Even before total income rises, Treasury would see some revenue offset to any net tax reduction.

Furthermore, national income would begin to grow faster right from the start. An extra point on the growth rate would add a cumulative extra half trillion dollars to federal revenues over seven years. There would also be gains on the spending side of the budget. More people working, and working at higher-paying jobs, would mean a natural reduction in claims for income support payments. These savings would mount with time.

Not all of the budget savings from faster economic growth and lower interest rates would be available in the first few years of the reform. But in light of the enormous potential benefits of reform to the economy, the population, and the budget, it would be reasonable to make a special effort to restrain the growth of federal spending to accommodate the change in the tax system.

Notes

1. A graduated rate variant of the savings exempt income tax comprises the individual tax portion of the Nunn-Domenici USA (Unlimited Saving Allowance) Tax proposal.

2. See Robert E. Hall and Alvin Rabushka, *The Flat Tax,* second edition (Stanford, California: Hoover Institution Press, Stanford University, 1995). Several variations on the approach have been offered by Representative Dick Armey and Senator Richard Shelby, Senator Arlen Specter, and others.

3. National sales taxes have been discussed or proposed by Senator Richard Lugar, House Ways and Means Chairman Bill Archer, and Representatives Bill Tauzin and Dan Schaefer, among others.

4. Value-added taxes, collected by businesses at each stage of production on the labor compensation they pay and the capital income they receive, and manufacturers' excise taxes are the least visible taxes of all. The commission did not give serious consideration to these taxes.

5. Border adjustability is often cited as an advantage of a national sales tax (or of other so-called indirect taxes, such as a VAT). However, most economists are skeptical that border adjustability would benefit the U.S. economy as a whole. It would not, by itself, increase total U.S. output and jobs. It would rearrange that output somewhat, and shift resources accordingly, but to no apparent purpose. We would produce more for export, and less for our own use, and we would import more to fill in the gap. The balance of payments would be largely unaffected, reflecting the same level of international

capital flows as before the changes. Jobs gained in producing for export would be at the expense of jobs aimed at production for domestic use. There would be adjustment costs due to the change in production patterns, and potential efficiency losses. Consumption-based taxes are not taxes on consumption. They are taxes on the labor and capital income earned in producing goods and services. The U.S. tax on workers and capital employed in the United States ought not to vary depending on where their products are sold. If Congress adopts a sales tax, consideration should be given to choosing the origin-based variety, which is the approach most consistent with simple territorial taxation.

6. Repayment of loans would be part of deductible net saving; borrowing would be a taxable inflow, but only if used for consumption and not repaid. Borrowing used to buy assets such as stocks, a home, or a machine for one's business would not result in more taxable income because the outlays would be deductible saving, canceling the effect.

7. Charitable contributions would be deductible by the donor. In theory, the recipients would take the contributions into income, but in practice, there is no need to. Charities either distribute their receipts to employees, researchers, students, or the poor, etc., or save a portion, all of which are deductible activities. The poor who receive charity would be too poor to owe tax. Current law simply allows the charitable deduction and ignores the remaining calculations.

In the pure form of this system, all payroll and state and local taxes would be deductible. State and local taxes are outflows. They largely fund welfare and other aid to the poor (income transfers akin to charitable contributions to persons below taxable levels of income) or education (a transfer that pays for the cost of the recipient's acquisition of human capital), all of which could be considered, in theory, to be reasonable deductions. Some state and local services accrue to the individual taxpayer or homeowner, however, and the amounts of these activities vary widely by states and localities. The tax literature is divided on this deduction.

8. More generally, in a pure version of this tax, businesses would not be taxable because their outflows would always equal their inflows. Business inflows would include the revenues from sales of goods and services and income on financial investments, plus borrowing and sales of new shares to stockholders. Their outlays would include operating costs (wages, purchases of materials, inventory, outlays on research and development, rent and royalties paid, etc.), taxes, dividend payments to shareholders, interest payments to lenders, and investment in plant and equipment. Anything left over for financial investment would be treated as tax-deferred saving on behalf of the shareholders.

State and local taxes are costs of doing business. If state and local taxes are disallowed as deductions, businesses would have to file tax forms just to pay federal tax on their state and local taxes. This system works best, and achieves the greatest degree of simplification, if all business expenses are deductible.

9. The version referred to is that introduced by Representative Armey, which modified the original Hall-Rabushka system to allow for the deductibility of pension contributions. Existing types of pension arrangements (deductible contributions, taxable benefits) would continue to be permitted under this bill, and may be liberalized.

10. The taxable income for financial institutions would be the difference between interest received and paid, less wages and other costs, as under current law. The problem arises because many of the charges and fees of financial intermediaries are contained in the spread between the interest rate they charge borrowers and the rate they pay depositors (or, for brokerages, the spread on securities transactions). If borrowers are not allowed to deduct interest paid to the intermediaries, special rules would be needed to tell the customers how much of the interest or other charges they paid constitute the "intermediation service" of the intermediary that is a deductible business expense.

11. Senator Arlen Specter (R-Pa) has introduced a version of this tax with these two adjustments.

12. Bipartisan Commission on Entitlement and Tax Reform, Final Report, Washington, D.C., January 1995.

For more information, contact:
Stephen J. Entin, Institute for Research on the Economics of Taxation, 1300 19th Street, N.W., Suite 240, Washington, D.C. 20036.
Phone: (202) 463-1400.

DEDUCTIONS AND TRADE-OFFS

Discussions of "tax reform" too often bypass the most basic structural questions, such as what should be taxed and what the tax rate should be, and jump ahead to the relatively peripheral issue of itemized deductions for individuals.

The controversy is not about whether or not deductions will be permitted in a new tax system. All plans for a new tax system would exempt low-income citizens in one way or another, through standard or specific deductions, personal exemptions, exclusions, adjustments or credits. With the exception of cash rebates or refundable tax credits (which are actually federal spending programs run though the tax code), the various ways of leaving some portion of income untaxed have essentially the same effect under a single tax rate.

The issues are (1) how large should the total of such deductions be, given the fact that having more deductions implies a higher tax rate; and (2) what form should the deductions take. Some prefer a larger "standard" deduction and/or personal exemption to specific "itemized" deductions. The issue is sometimes posed as if specific deductions are to be eliminated in order to get a lower tax rate, but that is not true if any revenue gained from eliminating specific deductions is devoted to enlarging the standard deduction. So long as the dollars involved are the same, then either form of deduction reduces the amount of income left to be taxed, and therefore keeps the tax rate higher than otherwise.

The Tax Reform Act of 1986 eliminated many specific deductions, such as a deduction for state and local sales tax, for individual health insurance premiums and for consumer interest expense. But this was matched by an increase in standard deductions and personal exemptions. The total of all deductions was 23.4 percent of adjusted gross income in 1990-92, up from 23.1 percent in 1982-84.[1] Only the form of deductions changed, not the amount.

A common concern is that unless all specific deductions are eliminated, then not one can be eliminated. The experience of 1986 suggests that this is not necessarily true. Several large deductions were eliminated or severely curtailed after 1986, while other specific deductions were not affected.

Simplicity.

Simplicity is not a very persuasive argument when it comes to choosing between standard or itemized deductions. In recent years, the I.R.S. has required detailed proof of small charitable contributions. Yet the largest itemized deductions, for taxes and mortgage interest, merely involve copying a number from one form to another and subtracting.

The real sources of complexity for individuals include keeping records on the buying and selling of houses, calculating the alternative minimum tax (AMT), calculating the amount of Social Security benefits subject to tax, calculating the phase-out of exemptions and deductions at higher incomes, reporting investment income, determining which interest expenses are deductible and which are not, and engaging in estate planning. All major plans for a new tax system would eliminate all of these major sources of tax complexity, regardless of whether any specific deduction was kept or not. All new tax plans would also eliminate the far greater complexities in defining and reporting business income, including complex depreciation schedules, AMT, and the elaborate system of taxes and credits on income produced abroad.

Fairness.

In the past, a major fairness argument has always been that itemized deductions or personal exemptions were more valuable to those in higher tax brackets. With a single tax rate, this objection becomes irrelevant, because deductions are equally valuable to all taxpayers.

People in similar circumstances should bear similar burdens. On this basis, it might be argued that some itemized deductions or exemptions are fair, because they measure income that people no longer have at their disposal (such as alimony payments or charitable contributions), or because they adjust for the fact that families with many children actually have a higher poverty threshold than smaller families with the same income.

Neutrality.

Another argument for getting rid of certain deductions and exclusions might be that they violate "neutrality," distorting the allocation of resources in ways that might harm the economy. Distortions have not often been mentioned in the context of the few remaining itemized deductions for individuals. Nobody complains, for example, that the deduction for charitable contributions causes too much generosity.

Some have argued that the mortgage interest deduction unduly favors investment in housing. "It is interesting," writes Robert Hall, "that although the personal tax treatment of interest on borrowing against securities is identical to that for houses, nobody has characterized the deduction of interest on securities as a 'subsidy' to securities." [2]

To the extent that the existing tax system has favored housing investment, it is largely because corporate investment is subject to so many layers of taxation. The fact that capital gains on houses can be rolled over into the same type of investments is not favoritism, except in comparison with the way other gains are now taxed. It is true that the shelter the home provides (measured by the "imputed rent" that GNP accountants assume homeowners "pay" themselves) is not taxed at the federal level, but it is taxed by the property tax.

Before the 1986 tax law, the individual deduction for sales tax was a source of complexity, involving adding-up a lot of receipts or using a rather arbitrary table that based estimated sales on income. To some degree this may mean that residents of states with no income tax pay higher federal taxes so that residents of states with high income taxes can claim a deduction. People with the same income are also treated differently depending on where they live. The fact that only income (and property) taxes are now deductible for individuals may induce states and cities to rely more heavily on the income tax, and less on the savings-neutral sales tax.

Visibility.

For businesses, state and local taxes are costs of producing income, and therefore are deductible expenses. In many communities, the property tax is used to finance services (such as trash collection) that are financed by deductible fees to private providers in other communities. Sales taxes on business materials and equipment are deductible, since they are part of other deductible costs of doing business. For individuals, state and local taxes are not costs of producing income, but to some degree, are the price of consumed public services. That price should be visible. Deductibility of certain state and local taxes may reduce the visibility of those taxes. However, some of the revenue raised by state and local taxation supports education and income transfers to the poor, which are tax-deductible transfers when achieved through private charities, and which represent the transfer of income from the taxpayer to the ultimate recipient of the income. This is a gray area requiring further study.

Symmetry.

The amount of revenue lost through deductions often depends on whether or not the operating principle of symmetry is maintained. With perfect symmetry, any deductible expense to one taxpayer would normally be taxable income to the person or company that receives that money. With a single tax rate, the net effect on revenue is roughly zero.

The mortgage interest deduction, for example, need not involve any significant revenue loss so long as symmetry is maintained—that is, so long as lenders are required to pay taxes on the interest income they receive.[3] One could retain current law practice—allowing homeowners to deduct their mortgage interest and requiring the lenders to pay tax on it—with little or no adverse effect on the tax rate. Not deducting the interest and not taxing it is somewhat simpler than deducting the interest and taxing it, but it yields very similar after-tax results for both borrowers and lenders. Under current law, mortgage lenders charge a rate that includes the tax they must pay on the interest, but borrowers save a corresponding portion of the interest rate because the interest they pay is tax deductible. Under the alternative treatment, the lender would charge a lower tax-free rate about equal to the after-tax rate borrowers face now.

Exclusions in current law violate several principles. Non-pension fringe benefits are labor costs that are deductible by the employer but are excluded from the taxable income of the employee (a violation of symmetry). Health care and cafeteria plans are the biggest examples. Excluding fringe benefits from taxable income makes them relatively more attractive than cash wages, leading people to buy more of the favored services and products than they otherwise would (violating neutrality and distorting output). The exclusion has led most working Americans to obtain health insurance for themselves and their families through employer-provided health plans. These plans hide a portion of workers' compensation, limit people's control over their health plans, and result in third-party payment systems that hide costs and lead people to treat health care as a (nearly) free good (violating visibility). The consequence is over-use of the health care system that drives up insurance costs for families and businesses and increases federal and state government outlays for health care for the poor and the elderly.

Each deduction, exclusion, adjustment, and tax credit needs to be held up against the principles of sound taxation and judged on its merits. The choice between standard and specific deductions is less important than the overall size of all types of deductions. If the public prefers that a large amount of revenue be devoted to deductions or exclusions, regardless of what form those deductions or exclusions take, then the tax rate must be higher than otherwise, or federal spending must be reduced.

Notes

1. I.R.S., *Statistics of Income (SOI) Bulletin,* Spring 1995, table 7, p. 178. The amount of "adjustments" to income did fall, however, from about 4 percent of AGI in 1985 to one percent by 1993, mainly because of tight restrictions on Individual Retirement Accounts after 1986.

2. Robert E. Hall, "The Effects of Tax Reform on Prices and Asset Values," paper presented to a National Bureau of Economic Research conference, Washington, D.C., November 7, 1995, p. 15.

3. Some portion of the interest might be received by foreigners not subject to withholding and by tax-exempt organizations.

For more information, contact:
Alan Reynolds, The Hudson Institute, 1015 18th Street, N.W., Suite 200, Washington, D.C. 20036. Phone: (202) 223-7775.

INCOME TAX TREATMENT OF PAYROLL TAXES AND SOCIAL SECURITY BENEFITS

The deduction, as allowed in current law, of the employer's half of the payroll tax as a business expense should be retained. Consideration should be given to allowing individuals to deduct their half of the payroll tax from taxable income as well. The increases in the 1993 budget agreement in the amount of social security benefits subject to income tax should be rolled back, and the method of taxing benefits in the future should be reformed. The social security earnings test should be eased or eliminated.

Retention of the employer's deduction would ease the transition to a new tax system by avoiding the need to alter existing labor contracts and compensation, and would avoid imposing a tax on a tax. A similar deduction for the employee's half would lower the burden of the tax on employment and labor income.

DEDUCTION OF PAYROLL TAXES AND AMOUNT OF BENEFITS TAXED

Under current law, the 15.3 percent payroll tax that supports the social security system is nominally levied half on employers and half on employees.[1] Employers may deduct their half of the payroll tax as a business expense (labor cost) in computing their taxable income under the income tax. Individuals are not allowed an itemized deduction of their half of the tax. The self-employed may deduct half of their payroll tax payments, corresponding to the employer's deduction. Since 1983, individuals and married taxpayers above certain incomes have had to pay tax on up to 50 percent of their social security retirement and disability benefits (corresponding to the half of the payroll tax contributions that had been deducted by employers). In the Omnibus Budget Reconciliation Act of 1993 (OBRA93), that percentage was increased to as much as 85 percent for upper-middle-ncome taxpayers.

It would make sense to treat the retirement and disability portion of the payroll taxes and social security benefits as if they were pension arrangements. Contributions should be deductible, and, ultimately, an appropriate portion of the retirement and disability benefits received should be taxable. Medicare taxes and benefits could be treated like private health insurance.

Current recipients of social security benefits should not have to pay tax on more than half of current benefits, because only half of the payroll taxes (the employer's share) collected on their earnings during their working years were deductible. Consequently, the percent of benefits subject to tax should be reduced immediately from 85 percent to 50 percent. If individuals are allowed to deduct the individual portion of the payroll tax in the future, then increasing amounts of retirement and disability benefits should eventually be subjected to tax. Because people now in the work force will not have been allowed such a deduction for a portion of their working lives, the amount of benefits potentially subject to tax should rise *very* slowly, increasing slightly for each new group of people reaching retirement age, and taking forty years (a working lifetime) to reach 100 percent.

Under current law and demographics, an increasing number of future retirees will receive less in benefits than they have paid in payroll taxes (in present value), and would be better off deducting the tax than escaping tax on the benefits.[2] Note, too, that current law is already increasing the taxation of benefits over time, even for current retirees (and without an additional deduction), because the income thresholds people have to reach before benefits are taxed are not indexed for inflation.

The Hall-Rabushka flat tax and its variations take the opposite approach to neutral treatment of the social security system. They eliminate the employer deduction for payroll taxes, and, correspondingly, eliminate all taxes on benefits. This is a theoretically equivalent approach over a working lifetime; the share of benefits taxed equals the share of payroll taxes deducted. However, the transition to that system would require altering current wage and salary agreements affecting all workers and businesses, and would provide a windfall to current beneficiaries on benefits corresponding to previously deducted taxes.

Going further in the other direction to allow both employers and employees a credit for payroll taxes would go well beyond normal treatment of pensions or saving. Folding the payroll tax into the income tax rate structure in this manner would require higher tax rates on wages, salaries, and the returns on private saving. There are other ways to deal with the problems posed by payroll taxes without raising the income tax rate structure to that degree. If further relief from the payroll tax is required, it would be preferable to allow individuals to redirect a portion of it into their own private retirement arrangements.[3]

REFORMING HOW BENEFITS ARE TAXED

Whatever percent of benefits is deemed taxable in the future, the current method of taxing the benefits must be scrapped. It is totally inconsistent with a single tax rate system, and is an outrage even under a graduated rate system. The current tax on benefits is really a tax on other retirement income—interest, dividends, pensions, annuities, and wages—at super-normal tax rates, as that other income exceeds certain thresholds. These super-normal tax rates are an extreme penalty on private saving and strongly urge young workers to avoid saving for retirement.

Retirees subject to the taxation of benefits must add $0.50 in social security benefits to taxable income for each dollar that their income exceeds $25,000 for single filers and $32,000 for couples, until half of benefits are taxed. They must add $0.85 to taxable income for each dollar of income over $34,000 for single filers and $44,000 for couples until 85 percent of benefits are taxed. Earning an extra dollar of interest, dividend, pension, or annuity income can add $1.50 or $1.85 to taxable income, effectively increasing marginal tax rates to 1.5 or 1.85 times normal levels. For someone in the 28 percent tax bracket, there is a marginal tax rate of 42 percent or 52 percent on an additional dollar of interest. On wages subject to the payroll tax, marginal tax rates can reach 56 percent to 65 percent. Rates can range from 85 percent to 115 percent on wages when the worker is also subject to the social security earnings test. (See below.) The income thresholds are not adjusted for inflation. By the time the baby boom finishes retiring, nearly all beneficiaries will be paying tax on some portion of their benefits.

The 50 percent and 85 percent phase-ins of benefits into taxable income should be eliminated to remove the spikes in the marginal tax rates. Whatever part of benefits should be taxable should simply be added to other taxable income. This should impose no hardship on those not paying tax on benefits under current law (a diminishing number over time as inflation erodes the thresholds) if personal- and family-exempt amounts under the income tax are raised to more generous levels under tax restructuring. If higher exempt amounts and reduced taxation of savings income under tax restructuring are not deemed sufficient to shelter lower income elderly taxpayers from taxation of benefits, either of two alternative allowances could be adopted. An additional exempt amount could be allowed for the elderly. Alternatively, some dollar amount of social security benefits, for example, $2,000 for a single retiree, $3,000 for a couple receiving the 50 percent spousal benefit, and up to $4,000 for a two-worker couple, could be made tax exempt. Benefits above the exempt amounts would simply be added to taxable income, up to the maximum taxable fraction in force for each age group.

EASING THE SOCIAL SECURITY EARNINGS TEST

Substantial increases in the social security earnings test, or its complete elimination, are essential to encourage continued contributions by the most experienced part of the labor force. Easing the earnings test would remove an enormous barrier to productive participation by persons age 62 through 69 in the labor force. It would enable them to raise their incomes, and would raise income and payroll tax receipts by more than it would increase government outlays. Everyone would gain.

The earnings test reduces social security benefits by one-third (for recipients ages 65–69) or one-half (for recipients ages 62–64) of wage and salary income in excess of very modest exempt amounts. These cuts are equivalent to 33.33 percent and 50 percent tax rates on the affected income, on top of income and payroll tax rates. At incomes of only $15,000 to $25,000, combined marginal tax rates on wages can reach 65 percent to 85 percent. At incomes of $25,000 to $60,000, taxation of benefits and the earnings test can generate marginal tax rates of 85 percent to 115 percent, blatantly confiscatory.

Notes

1. Of the total, 12.4 percent supports social security retirement and disability benefits, and 2.9 percent supports Medicare Part A hospital insurance benefits.

2. An alternative, more complicated approach to taxing benefits is to exclude an amount equal to the taxes individuals paid into the system, and tax the excess. This would be done on an "annuitzed basis"—a portion of each year's benefits, based on one's earnings history and life expectancy, would be attributed to tax payments, and the remainder would be taxable. For people who retired many years ago, and who will get back far more in benefits than they paid in taxes, the taxable share of benefits would be quite high. Future recipients will get back far less, relative to their tax payments, and would have a much smaller share of benefits subject to tax. The percentage would vary by individual, by marital status, and by generation.

3. See, for example, the discussion in the Final Report of the Bipartisan Commission on Entitlement and Tax Reform, Washington, D.C. January 1995.

For more information, contact:
Stephen J. Entin, Institute for Research on the Economics of Taxation,
1300 19th Street, N.W., Suite 240, Washington, D.C. 20036.
Phone: (202) 463-1400.

SIMPLIFY INTERNATIONAL TAXATION

Taxation of personal and business income earned abroad is a very complicated feature of the current income tax code. Congress should consider a territorial tax system to replace the global system in current law. That is, the U.S. tax should be imposed on all income generated within the borders of the United States, whether by U.S. residents or foreigners. Conversely, income earned outside the United States by U.S. businesses and individuals should be not be subject to U.S. taxes.[1]

Unlike most nations, the United States taxes the repatriated global income of its businesses that operate subsidiaries or partnerships abroad, after allowance of a tax credit for foreign income taxes paid. U.S. firms with operations in foreign countries owe tax on their repatriated earnings if the tax rate in the foreign country is less than that in the United States. U.S. individuals also owe U.S. tax on their interest or dividend income from foreign investments after a similar tax credit. Wages and salaries earned abroad by Americans are subject to similar treatment on amounts above $70,000. Conversely, the costs of some activities carried out in the United States are treated, for tax purposes, as if they were foreign, as with the complicated allocation rules regarding the cost of research and development.

The foreign tax provisions are among the most complex features of the U.S. tax code. They impose immense costs of compliance to U.S. taxpayers and very high enforcement costs to the IRS for only a small gain to the Treasury. The U.S. tax code would be simpler, and the income of U.S. residents would be greater, if the United States were to adopt territorial taxation.

The attempt to tax foreign earnings of U.S. businesses raises relatively little revenue. It merely discourages repatriation of business income earned abroad to the United States for reinvestment or distribution to shareholders or other owners. Firms do not repatriate their foreign earnings unless they have sufficient foreign tax credits to avoid the extra tax. Nonetheless, the damage done by the current system to particular U.S. businesses is substantial, in terms of high compliance costs and lost competitiveness.

The foreign tax provisions of the internal revenue code put U.S. businesses and individuals at a considerable competitive disadvantage in global markets, and generally reduce total world-wide investment by, and income of, U.S. residents. Other nations have income tax systems that are primarily territorial. They do not impose taxes on the foreign earnings of their resident businesses or individuals. Consequently, U.S. firms operating in a foreign country with corporate tax rates that are lower than in the U.S. are at a competitive disadvantage compared with firms from most European or Asian countries, because only the U.S. firms would owe a second layer of tax to the country in which its parent company is based. Similarly, American workers abroad in low-tax countries, and the companies that employ them, are at a disadvantage relative to foreign workers and firms in such locations.

The global tax system of the United States discourages U.S. firms from engaging in production or other activities abroad, or pressures U.S. businesses to structure foreign business operations in particular forms purely for tax reasons. This should not be a goal of tax policy. Imposing higher taxes on foreign operations of U.S. businesses does not improve the U.S. investment climate, and does not add to domestic investment. Insofar as it discourages investment abroad, however, it costs domestic U.S. operations billions of dollars in sales to potential foreign subsidiaries and partnerships that were never formed. In some cases, the opposite problem arises; other U.S. tax provisions sometimes force foreign subsidiaries to invest in foreign projects at the expense of U.S. projects to avoid additional U.S. taxes, clearly a perverse result.

In recent years, the United States has imported capital because investment has far exceeded domestic saving. The new, growth-friendly tax system, such as the commission has recommended, would undoubtedly encourage domestic saving, but it would probably attract foreign capital, too, by making the United States a particularly attractive place in which to invest. A capital-importing country may raise more revenue from a simple territorial tax system than from a system based on the residence of the investor.

Whatever new tax system is chosen, there must be a clearer, simpler, and more certain determination of what income is foreign or domestic, or what international transaction is taxable, than under current law. The current confusion over transfer pricing must be eliminated. In addition, attention must be given to the proper tax treatment of foreign source license fees and royalties so as not to discourage research and development in the United States.

Note

1. These results would occur naturally under an origin-based sales tax or VAT and a returns-exempt income tax, and could be designed into a saving-deferred income tax. The sales tax, VAT, and returns-exempt income tax would be collected at the business level before dividends and interest were paid to lenders and shareholders, including foreigners. Under the saving-deferred tax, in which businesses pass income on to lenders and shareholders for taxation, business payments to foreigners could be made subject to withholding, much like current law, so that they need not file tax returns. Interest payments to foreigners on federal government bonds do not represent returns on business investment or economic activity, and, as under current law, would not be subject to withholding. Destination-based sales taxes and VATs that rebate the tax at the border are not territorial.

For more information, contact:
Stephen J. Entin, Institute for Research on the Economics of Taxation, 1300 19th Street, N.W., Suite 240, Washington, D.C. 20036. Phone: (202) 463-1400; or Alan Reynolds, The Hudson Institute, 1015 18th Street, N.W., Suite 200, Washington, D.C. 20036. Phone: (202) 223-7775.

BIOGRAPHIES OF THE COMMISSIONERS

THE NATIONAL COMMISSION ON ECONOMIC GROWTH AND TAX REFORM

Chairman **JACK KEMP** is founder and current co-director of Empower America, a public policy and advocacy organization. Kemp served as Secretary of the U.S. Department of Housing and Urban Development in the Bush Administration, and represented the Buffalo, N.Y., area for 18 years in the U.S. House of Representatives. He played professional football for 13 years as quarterback for the San Diego Chargers and Buffalo Bills. His father was a small-businessman who helped start a trucking company in and around Los Angeles, California.

"If you tax something, you get less of it. If you subsidize something, you get more if it. The problem in America today is that we are taxing work, saving, investment, and productivity; and we're subsidizing debt, welfare, consumption, leisure, and mediocrity."

Vice Chairman **EDWIN J. FEULNER, JR.,** is president of the Heritage Foundation, a leading public policy group in Washington, D.C. He also serves as chairman of the Institute for European Defense and Strategic Studies in London. Feulner, who has a Ph.D. from the University of Edinburgh, served as consultant for Domestic Policy to President Reagan, and was the Chairman of the U.S. Advisory Commission on Public Diplomacy.

"Our tax code has become a complex web of penalties, disincentives, loopholes, and preferences. No amount of tinkering at the edges will save the system. The only answer is to replace it with a new system that rewards work, saving, and risk-taking."

LORETTA H. ADAMS started her professional career as a management trainee at the Panama City, Panama, Sears store on a $25-a-week salary. Ms. Adams later immigrated to the United States and went on to become founder of the San Diego–based Market Development, Inc., a consumer, marketing, and opinion research firm with nearly 100 employees. Since 1978, her company has serviced Latin-American consumers in the United States and Latin America and has become one of the top one hundred research firms in the country.

"The conditions that produced the current tax system no longer contribute positively to a twenty-first-century global economy. We now have the opportunity to create a tax system that is more responsive to our times, situation, and needs and, hopefully, we will grasp it fully."

J. KENNETH BLACKWELL lived in public housing for the first seven years of his life only to later pioneer housing reforms as the Deputy Undersecretary of the U.S. Department of Housing and Urban Development. Today, he serves as Treasurer of the State of Ohio, having previously held public office as a member of the Cincinnati City Council and mayor of Cincinnati. He is a member of the Council on Foreign Relations in New York, and previously served as U.S. Ambassador to the United Nations Human Rights Commission and as vice president of Xavier University in Cincinnati.

"There is something fundamentally wrong with a tax system that costs Americans $250 billion to comply. A simpler tax system would help break the chains that currently bind entrepreneurial spirit."

HERMAN CAIN learned the value of hard work from his father who concurrently worked three jobs—one of which was as a janitor at The Pillsbury Company in Atlanta. At age twelve, Herman went to work with his father at Pillsbury, helping him as "assistant janitor." Twenty-two years later Cain would become a Pillsbury vice president (computer systems) and later be selected as president of the firm's then-subsidiary company, Godfather's Pizza, Inc. In 1988, he successfully led a group of Godfather's Pizza, Inc. senior management in purchasing the chain from Pillsbury. He currently serves as chairman and CEO of Godfather's Pizza, Inc. Prior to his tenure at Godfather's, Cain worked for the U.S. Navy as a mathematician, the Coca-Cola

Company as a business analyst, and was an executive with Burger King Corporation.

"One of America's greatest strengths is its ability to change. . . . Our eighty-two-year-old tax 'mess' is long overdue for dramatic, sensible change."

CARROLL CAMPBELL served two four-year terms as one of the most popular and innovative governors in South Carolina's history. His legacy as governor includes government reform, record job expansion, net tax cuts, economic growth, and investment in his state. Campbell launched his political career in 1970, first serving in the state House and Senate and later in the U.S. Congress, where he served on the Banking, Appropriations, and Ways and Means committees. He also served as chairman of the National Governors' Association, the Republican Governors' Association, and the Southern Governors' Association, as well as Chairman of the Southern Growth Policies Board. Today he is president and CEO of the American Council of Life Insurance.

"The tax system should encourage investment and job creation, foster long-term savings, and increase the focus on individual and family economic responsibility. In short, tax policy should encourage long-term savings for retirement."

PETE DU PONT, during his tenure as governor of Delaware from 1977–1985, implemented a highly successful pro-growth tax policy by dramatically lowering marginal tax rates, causing the state's economy to boom and overall tax collections to jump, and enacting a constitutional amendment that limited both tax and state spending increases. He also served as a state legislator and Congressman and sought the Republican nomination candidate for President of the United States. He currently serves as policy chairman of the National Center for Policy Analysis, and writes a weekly column on public policy that is distributed to more than 400 newspapers across the nation.

"The men and women who spoke to us reflected an American consensus: Our tax system is destroying our opportunities. It's time to replace it."

JACK FARIS started working at age thirteen earning 50 cents an hour at his parents' service station. Faris learned early in life the challenges of running a small family business and the importance of hard work. After running his own business in Nashville, Tennessee, he became president and CEO of the National Federation of Independent Business (NFIB), the nation's largest small business advocacy organization with more than 600,000 members.

"Regulation and taxes are strangling small business on Main Street. Give us relief and we will create the jobs and build America's future for our children and grandchildren."

MATT FONG serves as Treasurer of the State of California. Prior to his election, Fong served as Vice Chairman of the State Board of Equalization, California's tax agency. Fong streamlined the agency, cutting millions of dollars of waste, reformed the state's tax code by sponsoring changes to the unitary tax, and made the agency more "taxpayer friendly." A graduate of the U.S. Air Force Academy currently holding the rank of Lt. Col. USAFR, he earned an MBA and law degree, started a small business, and worked for Sheppard, Mullin, Richtor and Hampton as a transactional corporate attorney.

"Too many Americans are sitting on the economic sidelines. A progressive single-rate flat tax will radically jump-start job creation, moving the unemployed off the sidelines to jobs."

THEODORE J. FORSTMANN is one of the most admired entrepreneurs in America with an unrivaled record of successful investments. Forstmann splits his time between running his firm, speaking out on behalf of economic opportunity and growth, and helping children worldwide. He has poured his energies and resources into leading relief efforts in Bosnia, sponsoring charities in South Africa, and funding scholarships and teaching students in America's inner cities. He is the senior partner of Forstmann Little & Co.

"The current tax system is ridiculously complicated, economically destructive, and morally corrosive. We desperately need a new tax code that puts the individual—not government—at the center of the equation."

DEAN KLECKNER took over the rented family farm in Iowa at the age of eighteen when his father died. Kleckner served in the Army and later returned to Iowa where he started out with a dozen sows, a dozen cows, and 300 chickens. Today he owns a 350-acre corn, soybean, and hog farm, and serves as President of the American Farm Bureau Federation, a post he has held since 1986. He also serves on the U.S. Advisory Committee on Trade Policy, a post to which he was first appointed by President Reagan, and reappointed by Presidents Bush and Clinton.

"Our tax system must be simple and equitable for all taxpayers, with no loopholes. It has to let hard-working taxpayers keep more of the money they have earned."

SHIRLEY PETERSON is president of Hood College in Frederick, Maryland. Prior to assuming the college presidency, she practiced tax law and also served as Commissioner of Internal Revenue under President Bush and Assistant Attorney General (Tax Division) at the U.S. Justice Department under President Bush. She was raised on a farm in Colorado.

"Citizens from around the country told us that the current law is too complex. This complexity breeds disrespect for the law and for our government. It's time to repeal the Internal Revenue Code and start over."

JOHN SNOW worked his way through college as a sports coach. Today he serves as chairman, president, and CEO of CSX Corporation in Richmond, Virginia, and has been with the company since 1977. Snow, who has a Ph.D. in economics from the University of Virginia and a law degree from George Washington University, also served as Deputy Undersecretary of the U.S. Department of Transportation, as a private attorney, and a college professor.

"The current tax system dims our prospects for the future and must be replaced by a new system for the twenty-first century which helps Americans to capitalize on opportunities—not stifle economic growth and entrepreneurial activity."

JOHN WIELAND always worked part-time growing up, from working at a gas station to delivering newspapers to stocking vending machines. Today, he is president of John Wieland Homes, Inc., of Atlanta, employing more than seven hundred full-time employees and thousands of subcontractors. For Wieland, success has meant the ability to give back to his community by providing housing for the working poor and working with Habitat for Humanity; he has served as a member of the International Board of Habitat.

"The consensus of the American people demands a completely new, simple, and fair tax code. Increased prosperity for all will be the outcome. The time is now."

TRC ADVISERS AND STAFF

Executive Director: *Grace-Marie Arnett*
Research Director: *Alan Reynolds*
Public Relations Counsel: *Richard Myers*
Senior Writer: *Jennifer Grossman*

ECONOMIC AND TECHNICAL ADVISERS

Stephen Entin, Institute for Research on the Economics of Taxation
Daniel Mitchell, Heritage Foundation
Stephen Moore, CATO Institute
Bruce Bartlett, National Center for Policy Analysis
Also, Arthur Hall, John Mueller, Judy Shelton, David Wentworth

STAFF OF THE NATIONAL COMMISSION ON ECONOMIC GROWTH AND TAX REFORM:

Elizabeth Kern
Scott Sundstrom
Also, Brian Pleva, Gilbert Pringle, Melinda Schriver

Tax advisers
Gary Gasper   *Donald Korb*
Jeanne Hoenicke   *Mark Weinberger*
Pamela Olson

Special Advisers:
Prof. Wayne Angell
Senator Robert Bennett (R-Ut)
Fred Goldberg
Dr. Norman Ture, Institute for Research on the Economics of Taxation

SPECIAL THANKS TO:

Grace Ann Leach and Anthony Fernandez
William Lehrfeld and Marie Jaeger
Burson-Marsteller: Tom Bell, CEO; Ken Rietz, Richard Moore
Also, Don Cunningham, Gene Grabowski, Laine McRaney,
    Maria Sheehan, Diane Tomb, and Preston Turner
Ziff-Davis Publishing Company: Eric Hippeau, CEO; Herbert Stern

LIAISONS TO THE MAJORITY LEADER AND SPEAKER:

Annette Guarisco
Kara Kindermann
Ed Kutler

LIAISONS AND ASSISTANTS TO COMMISSIONERS:

Frederick Ahearn	Barry Finkelstein	Karen Olson
Karen Asano	Arnold Havens	Christian Pinkston
Mary Blasinsky	Melba Kidd	Kathy Rowan
Robert Blatz	Ross Korves	John Shea
Denise Braye	Kent Knutson	Steve Spears
Ginny Bueno	Charles Kupperman	Patti Stinger
Jenny Camper	Dave Lane	Joan Trimble
Faye Chapman	Eileen Leach	Ken Vest
Susann Cole	Don Lipton	Mary Wallace
Virginia Correll	Jim Lucier	Jamie Wickett
Karen Coyle	Amy McClernan	Pat Wolff
Dave Cullen	Katy McGregor	Kathy Woodall
Stan Devereux	Veronica Montali	Alex Zarechnak
Jeff Dickerson	Grover Norquist	Sharon Zelaska
Tina Drennan	Ceci O'Connell	Brad Zuber
Mark Elam	Richard Odermatt	

The commission would not have been able to do its work without the dedicated and expert assistance of these people who volunteered their time and talents. And finally, thank you to the many people who provided financial support, to our witnesses, to those who wrote us, and to the hundreds of others who helped facilitate our work.

MEMBERS OF THE NATIONAL COMMISSION ON ECONOMIC GROWTH AND TAX REFORM

JACK KEMP
Chairman of the Commission
Co-Director
Empower America

EDWIN J. FEULNER
Vice Chairman of the Commission
President
The Heritage Foundation

LORETTA ADAMS
President
Market Development, Inc.

J. KENNETH BLACKWELL
Treasurer
State of Ohio

HERMAN CAIN
Chairman and CEO
Godfather's Pizza, Inc.

CARROLL A. CAMPBELL
President and CEO
American Council of Life
Insurance
*Former Governer of South
Carolina*

PETE DU PONT
Policy Chairman
National Center for Policy Analysis
Former Governer of Delaware

JACK FARIS
President
National Federation of
Independant Business

MATT FONG
Treasurer
State of California

THEODORE J. FORSTMANN
Founding Partner
Forstmann Little & Co.

DEAN R. KLECKNER
President
American Farm Bureau Federation

SHIRLEY D. PETERSON
President, Hood College
Former IRS Commissioner

JOHN SNOW
Chairman, President, and CEO
CSX Corposration

JOHN WIELAND
President
John Wieland Homes, Inc.

SCHEDULE AND THEMES OF TAX REFORM COMMISSION HEARINGS

Tax Reform Commission:
1133 Connecticut Avenue, N.W., Suite 1010, Washington, D.C. 20036.

JUNE
Wed., June 14 Launch meeting in Washington; News conference to introduce commissioners

Wed., June 28 Hearing in Washington: *"Review of major alternative proposals"*

JULY
Wed., July 12 Hearing in Washington: *"Compliance costs and burdens"*

Wed., July 19 Hearing in Boston: *"The Massachusetts experience with economic growth and tax reform"*

Wed., July 26 Hearing in Washington: *"Promises and pitfalls of comprehensive tax reform: Views of the American people"*

AUGUST
Wed., Aug. 2 Hearing in Omaha, Nebraska: *"The perspective from the farm community, business and industry"*

Wed., Aug. 16 Hearing in Charlotte, North Carolina: *"Entrepreneurship; State and local taxation; International competitiveness"*

Tues., Aug. 22 Hearing in Palo Alto, California: *"Creating new businesses and industries: The view from Silicon Valley"*

SEPTEMBER
Wed., Sept. 6 Hearing in Washington, D.C.: *"Views on the economics of taxation; Perspective on real estate"*

Fri., Sept. 8 Hearing in South-Central Los Angeles: *"Impact of tax policy on minority businesses and access to capital"*

Wed., Sept. 20 Hearing in New York City: *"From Harlem to Wall Street: Perspectives on inner-city entrepreneurship"*

Tues., Sept. 26 Hearing in Washington, D.C.: *"The impact of tax reform on inner-city business development"*

Wed., Sept. 27 Hearing in Cleveland: *"Historical perspectives on tax reform; Business and individual taxpayer concerns"*

OCTOBER–NOVEMBER–DECEMBER
Commission meetings to develop recommendations and report

JANUARY 17, 1996
Release of Tax Reform Commission recommendations